DEA LOHER: THREE PLAYS

Dea Loher

DEA LOHER: THREE PLAYS

Translated by David Tushingham

OBERON BOOKS
LONDON

WWW.OBERONBOOKS.COM

First published in 2014 by Oberon Books Ltd
521 Caledonian Road, London N7 9RH
Tel: +44 (0) 20 7607 3637 / Fax: +44 (0) 20 7607 3629
e-mail: info@oberonbooks.com
www.oberonbooks.com

Contents

Introduction   7

Olga's Room   13

Innocence   63

Land Without Words   155

'You Just Have To Deal With It'

The German theatre is traditionally a literary theatre. It was established relatively late, in the eighteenth century, in the courts of small principalities, as – in Schiller's words – 'the moral institution', a place of enlightenment and culture.

Goethe, Schiller, J.M.W. Lenz, Else Lasker-Schüler, Marieluise Fleisser, Bertolt Brecht...

These are just some of the substantial literary figures who have contributed to the development of German playwriting in the last 250 years. They are also, coincidentally, all writers who have given their names to playwriting prizes won by Dea Loher, whose work most clearly represents the continuity of this tradition into the present day.

The volume you are holding is the first collection of her works to be published in English and contains just three of the nineteen plays she has had performed since her debut in 1992.

Dea Loher was born in 1964 in Traunstein, Bavaria, an area renowned for its idyllic landscape near the German/Austrian border. Her father was a forester and in describing her family home she has mentioned that where some families have bookshelves, hers had a gun rack. Like many bookish children who grow up in areas renowned for their idyllic landscape, as soon as she was old enough, she left home and moved to the city, first to Munich where she studied literature and philosophy and then, after graduating and spending a year travelling in Brazil, to Berlin, just after the wall had come down, a metropolis in waiting and the epicentre of the improvised social experiment which was German reunification.

She planned to become a journalist. But then something distracted her. She saw an advertisement for a creative writing course, a course in dramatic writing led by Heiner Müller. She applied and to her surprise and delight was accepted. Suddenly she had to write a play, quickly. Drawing in part on her Brazilian experiences, she decided to write about Olga Benario, a German revolutionary whom the Brazilians had deported to Nazi Germany and had subsequently died in a concentration camp, a woman who no-one in Traunstein had ever heard of, but who was famous in East Germany as a heroine of the resistance to fascism, with streets and kindergartens and many other public institutions named after her.[1]

Right from the beginning, Dea Loher was instinctively drawn to powerful emotions and substantial themes. In common with many of her later plays, she places characters on stage at key points in their lives, characters who ask serious questions about what these lives mean, both to themselves and others. However, in an early interview she stresses that her principal concern when planning a new play is not subject matter, but language:

'I don't go looking for exciting subjects. You can't actually choose your own themes. For me the theatre is a space for language. If the language already expresses what people are feeling, this generates a kind of TV realism and that's boring. In the theatre language has to create characters and not the other way round.'[2]

Olga's Room is two kinds of play in one. It makes an explicit and formal contrast between narrative and action, between epic and dramatic theatre, between monologues and scenes. As Olga sits in solitary confinement in Ravensbrück concentration camp, she remembers moments from an earlier life in another prison on the other side of the world. Her detention in Brazil was similar in that it was also politically motivated and offered little chance of a favourable outcome, but it was a place where she was not alone, there were others who shared the same fate, and there was also an interrogator, a direct confrontation with the way of thinking responsible for her detention. In both the scenes and the monologues, language is Olga's way of working out where she is and how she got there, of keeping hold of her identity and of attempting to articulate some sense of hope.

In an awards acceptance speech in 2006 (this one was for the Bertolt Brecht Prize), Dea Loher commented:

'One of the main motivations for my writing is both an impulse and a narrative motif for my characters: creating a memory, ripping things away from forgetfulness, remembering in order to have a future. Writing means looking for connections, explanations, hypotheses, sometimes searching for lost truths, but this search becomes valuable when it uses reality as a springboard to open up

---

1   While I was preparing this introduction, Dea Loher wrote to me from Rio de Janeiro, expressing her horror at the fact that the city has a square named after Filinto Müller.

2   Interview with Eva Heldrich in programme for *Tattoo*, Berlin 1993

spaces which only exist in language and extend our sense of what is real. I would call it an 'open memory'; - a constructive one, which looks ahead, facing into the future, which takes the past as its source and the present as its field of play. Writing as both research into and design for people living together.'[3]

This search is already evident in *Olga's Room.*

By the time she wrote *Innocence* (first performed in 2003) Loher's writing had matured considerably. She had had the good fortune to find a director with whom she had been able to establish a regular working relationship, Andreas Kriegenburg, and a theatre (or more correctly a series of theatres run by the same Artistic Director, Ulrich Khuon, in first Hannover, then Hamburg and more recently Berlin) which was prepared to commission new plays from her consistently and then produce them on the main stage. Her collaboration with Kriegenburg was particularly important as not only did she have someone she could trust to realise her work in an imaginative and charismatic form but together they experimented with new methods of creating contemporary plays, writing the whole of the text during the rehearsal period or producing an entire series of short plays over the course of a season.

Andreas Kriegenburg's own background was very different to Dea Loher's. He had grown up under the socialist regime in East Germany and had not studied at a university. His first job had been as a stage hand and carpenter at his local theatre in Magdeburg. As a director and designer he was a very practical theatrical visionary. What they shared was the experience of living in a newly evolving hybrid Germany of 're-unification', a prosperous nation whose economic health did not apparently benefit many of its population but which served as an attractive destination for others, and a society where ideology continued to live in the memory while lacking any more active role.

Innocence – a title which could apply to any of the three plays in this volume – can be regarded as another experiment. It is a large-scale work with no protagonist, a collection of unlikely but plausible stories (several of the scenes are actually based on real-life events) which all take place in the same city. The various narratives: of the illegal immigrants who want to save a woman from drowning but hesitate in case they will have to explain themselves to the police,

3   Augsburg, 16th July 2006

of the pole dancer who can't see her audience because she is blind, of the fortune found in a plastic carrier bag at a bus stop, of the one-night-stand which turns into a suicide attempt, of the philosopher whose life's work turns out to be irrelevant, are all juggled with great confidence and considerable skill. Unlike *Olga's Room*, there is little in *Innocence* which is specifically German – the same events could take place in any major port in western Europe – but this in itself is an interesting observation or comment on how Germany was moving on from being a country very much moulded by its efforts to deal with its past and trying to play a more active part in the wider world.

This is even more true of *Land Without Words*, a text written in the voice of an artist who has recently visited the city of K, which both describes and demonstrates the unsettling effect of this extreme experience on her work and her thinking. It was based on a visit Dea Loher herself made to Afghanistan to teach at Kabul University. This was a very difficult experience:

'The Afghanistan experience was and is so radical for me because firstly actual reality there is so overpowering that it seemed impossible for me to transform it into a form of fictional literature – which would have been my task – and secondly because its pointlessness was so fundamental, that it destroyed every form of writing – even the attempt to "only" report it. This is – I have no other way of describing it – a pointlessness which seeps into words themselves and leaves them empty of meaning.

I don't know if this is something you will be able to comprehend. Because I can talk about it, now, and yet I still have the same feeling, and I think this state will persist, as if I am unable to grasp its essential nature. This is a paradox I have to live with.

I also don't know whether the fact that a lot of soldiers return from wartime service or so-called post-conflict countries and do not speak about their experiences is linked to this. Apart from the fact that they are dealing with the shock of traumatic experiences. But it must also have something to do with language getting lost. The original: absence of words. The loss of a limb in which meaning is constructed: the ordering and playful application of language. Something which is taken for granted is destroyed. The normal procedure, the security of being able to express what I feel and experience in words, is destroyed.'[4]

4   Acceptance speech for Bertolt Brecht Prize, as above.

Land Without Words was not an easy text to write. It took Dea Loher over a year after her visit to Kabul to make up her mind to write it. The form of the text is very open. There are no indications of cast or setting and an absolute minimum of punctuation. It is language in its purest form. What this language talks about is evidence of this author's curiosity about the world, her dedication to searching for truth and the depth of her moral concern accompanied at the same time by a keen scepticism: a willingness to ask awkward questions and come up with uncomfortable answers. As the artist says: 'you just have to deal with it.' This is what Dea Loher does. She engages with the world and turns the results into texts for the theatre. What else would we want a playwright to do?

David Tushingham

PLAYS BY DEA LOHER
In order of first performance

1992	*Olga's Room*
1992	*Tattoo*
1993	*Leviathan*
1995	*Stranger's House*
1997	*Bluebeard – Hope of Women*
1998	*Adam Geist*
1999	*Manhattan Medea*
2000	*Klara's Relationships*
2000	*Berlin Story*
2001	*Scissors*
2001	*Anna and Martha*
2001	*Storehouse of Happiness*
2002	*War Zone*
2003	*Innocence*
2004	*Life on the Praça Roosevelt*
2007	*Land Without Words*
2008	*The Final Fire*
2010	*Thieves*
2012	*Black Lake*

OLGA'S ROOM

Olgas Raum had its premiere at the Ernst-Deutsch-Theater Hamburg on 7 August 1992, directed by Ives Janseen.

This translation was first performed on 7 November 2012 at Centre Culturel de Rencontre Abbaye de Neumünster, Luxembourg and in the UK on 9 January 2013 at Arcola Theatre, London with the following cast in order of appearance.

OLGA BENARIO	Bethan Clark
GENNY	Sheena May/Larisa Faber
FILINTO MULLER	Pete Collis
ANA LIBRE	Ceridwen Smith

CREATIVE TEAM

Director	Samuel Miller
Design	Matt Sykes-Hooban
Lighting Design	James Smith
Sound Design and additional composition	Edward Lewis
Songs	Ewen Moore
Action Advisor	Rachel Bown-Williams of RC-Annie

PRODUCTION TEAM

Stage Manager	Nathalie Gunzlé
Production Manager	Ina Berggren
Press	Charlotte Donachie
Publicity Image	Grzegorz Rekas www.iconsdg.com
Trailer	www. acapmedia.co.uk

Characters

OLGA BENARIO

GENNY

ANA LIBRE

FILINTO MÜLLER

GUARDS, MEDICAL ORDERLIES

Monologue I

Duet I: Inventio

Monologue II

Pas de diable I

Monologue III

Trio I: Accusatio

Monologue IV

Pas de diable II

Monologue V

Pas de diable III

Monologue VI

Duet II: Negatio

Monologue VII

Trio II: Dementia

Monologue VIII

Quartet

Monologue IX

Exitus

MONOLOGUE I

I am Olga. This is my room. A cell in Ravensbrück concentration camp. How long have I been here? How long will I stay here, I don't know. We're writing the third year of the war. As long as the war lasts, I, Olga, will be staying here. The war can last a long time.

Be-na-rio. B E N A R I O. Born in 1908. That makes me 34 now. O L G A. In thin letters I carve my name in the walls. I scratch a map into my wall, a landscape of the whole world that surrounds me and in the distant continents I carve the places where I was and am imprisoned: 42 41 40 39 Ravensbrück concentration camp. 39 38 Lichtenburg concentration camp. 38 37 36 Berlin women's prison. 36 prison in Rio de Janeiro, Brazil.

I was handed over by the Brazilian police to the Gestapo, why. Don't let your memory be destroyed. Only if I can remember exactly will I experience the future. Prison. Grey walls. I talk to myself to stop going mad. I show myself pictures, tell myself stories. Here in my head is my album of memories. Remember one event every day and reconstruct it exactly.

That's the day that I joined the outlawed Communist youth movement. Name date of birth father mother nationality: – Jewish. – Nationality: – German. – That's Comrade Otto Braun, I went with him from Munich to Berlin to work underground for the CP. I was 17. And he was my lover.

Keep a cool head now. Don't let memories deceive me.

That is Luis Carlos Prestes. A Brazilian. Knight in shining armour. Leader of the armed resistance in his country. Against the dictatorship. After the years of struggle 24 25 26 27 disappeared. Went

to Moscow. Into exile. – The father of my child. –
Moscow: the only place I lived for any length of
time without being in prison. Even my child was
born in prison. Anita. Names, names, don't let
the evidence be wiped away. I had to leave Berlin
because. The party sent me into exile to Moscow
because. I save the past. I save my mind. I save
my life. I save myself.

Moscow 1934. Prestes belongs to the executive
committee of Comintern. My going with him to
Brazil, to resume the struggle which has already
been fought before, is not an order. But it is a
mission.

One year after I arrive I'm back inside a cell there.
I share a cell with Genny. She's Romanian. She's
young. Seventeen. Accused of political subversion.

DUET I: INVENTIO

GENNY   I can't stand the silence any longer. Will the waiting never end. They're forcing us to wait. Speak, Olga, talk so I forget my fear. I'm afraid of Filinto's guards, I'm afraid they're going to be coming for me next time. Perhaps nothing will happen to me. Perhaps I will be spared. And nothing must happen to you either. You've got to protect me. What's going to become of me if something happens to you? Talk, Olga, give me a talisman of words no one can take away. Words I can hide under like a vast coat, like in a forest. No one will find me and I will live in safety. I'm afraid, fear has already eaten a hole in my head, it's anaesthetized me so nothing bothers me any more. Tell me again, talk about before.

OLGA   I'll start with Berlin. I was a little bit older than you and lived in Berlin.

GENNY   Alone?

OLGA   Not alone. The man I lived with was Otto Braun.

GENNY   Did you love him?

OLGA   In those days –

GENNY   Go on.

OLGA   We were both working. For the Communist Party. He was an official, I earned money as a

GENNY   – Typist.

OLGA   – Secretary.

GENNY   Go on. Being arrested. Being released.

OLGA   We used to meet regularly in a tiny pub. In Neukölln. Workers. Talked. Read. Passed on information. Strikes. Protests.

GENNY   And then –

OLGA   They arrested both of us. 'Treason' for Otto Braun. I was an accomplice apparently in a campaign to dispossess the nobility. They couldn't prove

	anything. I was in Moabit for two months. Otto Braun spent eighteen months waiting for trial. We freed him. Six of us. From the courtroom.
GENNY	With guns?
OLGA	They weren't loaded. They were looking for us. We escaped to Russia with false passports.
GENNY	Your picture was in all the newspapers.
OLGA	I learnt Russian. Stood up in a lot of halls and made speeches. Was elected to the Central Committee.
GENNY	He –
OLGA	Otto Braun left. Another woman. She had time for him.
GENNY	The bastard. Forget Otto. Drum roll. Now it's time for Luis Prestes. Drum roll. Tell me about Luis Prestes.
OLGA	On a Winter's day in Russia I'm summoned by Dimitri, our Party Secretary, Manuilski. Quickly and quietly, without expressing any emotion, he asks me what I think of the struggle. Resistance, it's called, the people's struggle in South America. I say yes, yes, if a time has come, then there – to be honest I didn't think the time had come yet and I would have been happy if he'd sent me to Germany, back to Berlin, to gag Hitler's mouthpieces till they choked on their own brown drivel. But that's not what Manuilski asks me about. Prestes, in exile in Moscow, was desperate to go back to Brazil and topple the government of the dictator Vargas. The mission: I was to accompany Luis Carlos Prestes personally, to guarantee his safety. The Secretary gives me time to think.
GENNY	People say that you and Prestes, you met at a ball in Moscow, on an ice cold Winter night, with such a deep frost on the windows you couldn't see through them any more, one layer of frosty flowers growing over another. You all had red cheeks from

dancing and practically nothing on, because the ballrooms were heated by wood-burning stoves. It was so hot that little beads of sweat ran down the ladies' cleavages and the men's trousers stuck tight around the seat, but outside, outside it was so icy that it almost cracked the window panes.

OLGA I'd already heard about him, Captain Luis Carlos, the knight in shining armour, leader of Prestes' column, whose men were guerilleros in Brazil during the dictatorship. I was a parachutist myself in Moscow, learnt to fly, was well on the way to becoming the best fighter, paramilitary, they had in Russia. One day, as usual, I jumped – ten thousand five thousand two thousand metres free fall –, it was on this day after my jump that I met the captain from Bolivia in the casino; he described the captain from Brazil like this: he's as strong as a python that can wrap itself round a calf and break its spine with the movement of a single muscle, as courageous as the spotted jaguar, the onça pintada, and as agile as the tatú, the armadillo, at the same time an astute tactician, yet before the battle when every step of the attack has been fixed, a saint: he addresses his men and folds their hands in the most unremitting prayer which ever reached God's ear; in other words putting the most wrinkled five fingers round the barrel of a gun. They completed a legendary twenty five thousand kilometers before going their separate ways and escaping abroad. That's what he said. I had to laugh: was I supposed to believe these local myths, the whole of South America united in admiration – the time of heroes is long gone, the Bolivian wanted to write history.

GENNY It was a sign. A sign from Heaven. No, I'm not superstitious, God preserve me. *(She crosses herself.)* But it's fate. You had to fall in love with him, simply because of the Bolivian's words. They had this power.

OLGA	I wasn't thinking about that. I doubted…
GENNY	The first time you saw each other – you were standing in the ballroom, he came in through a doorway –, two pairs of eyes, lightning, electricity, magnetism, nothing could save you. They say it was at that ball and from then on you never wanted to be parted. And you wouldn't have been able to even if you'd wanted to. Inseparable. The party is the first to know: if we send her with him, she'll be his lover – his personal companion –, they each have no equal. Your love had no equal.
OLGA	*(Very cool.)* I've already told you, it was in the Comintern headquarters. An almost empty room, one desk in front of a bare wall, on the right an uncurtained window with a view out onto the streets. Manuilski didn't say a word, he gave me an inquiring look, I nodded.
	And with that he let Prestes into the room. He was a short, gentle man, very gaunt, he gave me a soft, dry handshake and looked hesitantly into my eyes.
GENNY	Then – honeymoon in Stockholm, Amsterdam, Paris, a luxury steamer to New York, only the best suites in the best hotels, flying across the Andes to South America – Lima, Buenos Aires, then Säo Paulo, and finally Rio, Rio…
OLGA	On the run, hiding, under cover. – Never taking the direct route, always in secret. They're looking for me in Germany and they're looking for Luis in Brazil. False names, altered faces. – No place is safe, not a moment's peace, no thought is finished – on the run, hiding, under cover. – Every day is different. – The only thing that stays the same is deception. – Every day on the run, hiding, under cover. That's over. They caught him with me and me with him. It's over now. *(She laughs.)* Hiding. We're both stuck in the cells.

GENNY   *(Sings.) Ah, se tu soubesses*
         como sou tão carinhoso,
         e que tanto que te quero,
         sincero o meu amour…

         [Oh if only you knew,
         how loving I am,
         how much I want you,
         how noble my love is…]

Blackout.

A clock ticking.

MONOLOGUE II

How the revolution came about. 34 Rio de Janeiro: The left form an alliance for national liberation. Freedom from dictatorship. Prestes becomes chairman. 35 Rio de Janeiro: the government outlaws the national liberation movement. There is unrest. We call for revolution. The government announces a state of emergency. And mobilizes its troops. The revolution collapses as quickly as it broke out. It is beaten down. Mass arrests. In searching for the leaders the Brazilian police receive help from the Intelligence Service. And the Gestapo.

They launch interrogations. Prestes is sentenced first to 17, then to a further 30 years imprisonment, that makes 47 years. Those who used to be guerilleros have changed sides and now execute their former comrades. The Chief of Police is called Filinto Müller. I don't know him well yet. Not well enough yet. But I know a few things about him. That years ago he used to fight for Prestes. For the revolution. And was decorated for bravery.

Filinto Müller is my interrogator. I want to deceive him for as long as possible. To confuse him with different faces and not give myself away. But Filinto won't listen to any stories. And he doesn't tell any stories. I have to be extremely reticent. Careful. Don't be afraid. Don't show it. I'm saving the past I'm saving my mind I'm saving my life I'm saving myself. I have no fear. I am not a victim. Just don't believe the torturer. Give nothing away under torture. Not a word. Silence.

PAS DE DIABLE I

FILINTO   Apparently you're pregnant.

OLGA   Yes, I am.

FILINTO   The Gestapo is well informed about you. You know how Hitler likes to keep an eye on Communist agents, you Jew. I can hand you over any time.

OLGA   I'm married to Prestes. I'm a Brazilian citizen. I am going to become the mother of a Brazilian child. According to the law of your country you can't hand me over.

FILINTO   You're lying. Your passport's a forgery. You've got no marriage certificate. You're a slag, a whore Prestes grabbed out of the gutter to satify himself on, slut. Hitler demands a sacrifice from you, from every Jew a Jewish sacrifice. Perhaps he'll just take your child away and let you live. You'll have to sacrifice your child to Herr Hitler. *(He laughs.)*

OLGA   I can't be transported. I'm pregnant. I'm malnourished. I spit blood at night. I'd never reach Germany alive. The child would die with me.

FILINTO   Who's crying about that? One whore's son less. *(He laughs.)* Your child. *(He laughs.)* How do I know you're really pregnant? That this child isn't the invention of your sick Jewish brain, that you're not going to suddenly lose it? That this is Prestes' child and not from one of the sweaty niggers who crawl out at night like rats from the latrines and beg you: make lust with me, come on, give it to me and you, you doll woman, vibrating, electrified, without morals or decency, you enjoyed it, shaking on a stick like a hollow scarecrow, blown about by the hot wind, inflated, till you're becalmed, lust diminishes, she sighs with fatigue, never any will power, she doesn't think, just bodies... bodies... *(He laughs.)*

OLGA	*(Assured.)* I demand a doctor. I demand a medical examination. And don't fool yourself. My name is still in the papers. I'm a foreigner. They care about what happens to me. I want to be taken to a public, to a city hospital. I want to be examined there.
FILINTO	Excellent idea. An excellent idea, this examination. Remember to remind yourself later on that it's what you wanted. I'll examine you myself, to make things simpler. No need to be afraid, I've got a lot of experience. *(He laughs.)* I'll do the toad test on you. *(He laughs.)* The toad test to detect early stages of pregnancy. A 99% success rate. Lies don't get very far. *(He laughs.)* When's the last time you bled? When's the last time you expelled your worthless, unfertilized egg, that slimy lump of blood, when? Answer! *(Pause.)*
OLGA	I already told you. I'm in the second month. The second month.
FILINTO	*(Laughs.)* Good. Very good. *(Lecturing.)* The test can be carried out successfully ten to twelve days after a missed period. *(Pause.)* In the morning you will go to the latrine and pass water. Take your enamel cup or your plate and piss into it. You'll bring me your steaming urine. I'll give you a toad, you put it between your hands. It's a male toad, a man. He sits on your lap. You've got to hold him tight, the lie detector. *(He laughs.)* Better than any lie detector. *(He laughs.)* I can also take a bit of blood from you. You give him your morning urine or your blood, they're both equally good to him. Let's take the urine. I inject your urine into the toad, the male toad gets to drink your yellow juice; food for his flesh, his blood, his lust. You sit there and hold on to him. Feel the toady skin against the palms of your hands, the tiny hard, warty bumps. It will take six hours. You will feel the male toad change: his lungs pump harder, his pupils dilate, his body

swells up rhythmically, his skin warms and softens, his warts become sharper and harder. – If you're really pregnant, he will shoot his sperm into your lap. – *(He laughs.)* After six hours he'll spray his sperm onto your lap. Toad jelly. *(He laughs.)*

OLGA   I'll piss on you. You can give your toad as much of my blood as you want. You can get me to talk, yes, but I'm going to talk about you, always talk about you, without stopping.

FILINTO   But – my little experiments are so harmless. Scientifically approved methods. Specialists use them, experts. Another suggestion then. I'll even let you choose the type of examination. – Do you know the dwarf carp method?

OLGA   No. No, I don't know it. I do not know it and I don't want to hear anything about it. I don't want to hear anything.

FILINTO   Oh but, you're going to listen, dear Olga, you are going to listen, whether you want to or not. The dwarf carp experiment is very pretty, really delightful. You'll like it. It even satisfies – aesthetic demands. *(He laughs.)* We wait until you're in the third or fourth month. We'll have two dwarf carp, a pair. The male has a glistening silky skin of green scales. I inject a sample of your urine under his skin. If you're expecting a boy, the dwarf carp will change the colour of its scales. Pretty, don't you think? A living sex indicator. His coat will turn steel blue, with a luminous orange tinge. *(He laughs.)* And we do the control experiment with the female: if you've got a girl growing in your belly then the female fish's egg-laying tube will grow by an inch *(Makes an obscene gesture.)*, it'll grow by an inch. *(He laughs.)* If you wish, dear Olga, you can eat the carp afterwards. You'll have them fried, on silver foil, served with a knife and fork, a fish knife and fork, and with potatoes and melted butter and their colours will shimmer and the egg-laying tube will stick up all brown and crispy. *(He laughs.)* You're a good actress, Olga Benario. Pregnant women are quick to feel sick, aren't they? They're so sensitive. Those surrounding them are expected to show consideration. Well I've heard a lot of people talk about the sickness associated with this condition. But doesn't it occur mostly first thing in the morning?

OLGA You're a pig, Filinto. You disgust me. What do you want from me? What am I supposed to do? Do you like doing it with pregnant women? Or does my resistance arouse you? Am I not worthless, a prisoner, a piece of body. Am I not too ill for you yet? I crap on you, Müller. I crap on you and your dirty life. I am a broken fragment. You'll get blood on your hands before you own me.

FILINTO No, I won't, Olga. I won't. I could crush you into tiny little pieces. Every day here I see strong bodies and how they break. I break them. But I don't want to crush you, not yet. You've got to want me, Olga Benario. I want you to learn to love me. You've got to desire me more than – Luis Prestes. I'm strong, Olga. There have been times I've loved five or six women in a night, sometimes just three; I've got pretty good... muscles. I've still got them. The women couldn't handle it, they couldn't bear so much strength, so much power. Some died groaning, others burst with swollen bellies, another one died of consumption. She could neither sleep or eat, all she could think of was my bed. *(He laughs.)*

OLGA And you think that's what I would crave? You must be sick, Filinto, sick and mad. I despise you. No, I don't despise even you but I understand what Prestes said about you: cowardly opportunist. Upstart. Traitor. And do you know why? You know why!

FILINTO	Luis Prestes is dead to you. He no longer exists. I destroy him. I am your master now. What can you know that I don't know? You will tell me everything. You will trust me. You and the child. My wife and my child. Who I take care of. Who I am responsible for.
OLGA	Prestes told me a lot about you. I know more about you than you think. I know you better than you imagine. You'd like to hide it, you're scared more people might find out, you want to undo the fact it ever happened: you – were a Captain in Prestes' column, one of the bravest men in the resistance, you were a guerillero yourself!
FILINTO	No. No. I am brave. I'm brave. I fought and won and was promoted and praised and people slapped me on the shoulder and liked saying my name.
OLGA	You fought against government troops, against the dictatorship. You were promoted to Major for your successes, for your distinguished service to Prestes' column.
FILINTO	Yes. Yes. I was a Major. And now I'm more than that. I have prisons full of prisoners, my prisoners. Before I owned nothing. Now I see dozens of them every day on their knees before me. They all love me, because I let them feel humility and what it means to experience mercy, to have their consciences relieved through absolution, to have their souls liberated, their crimes forgiven. They should love me because I know the truth about them, I discover the truth about every one of them. They have to reveal themselves to me. I am their God. Who did anyone love more fervently than their *lord*?
OLGA	You slipped off in the night like a coyote who's afraid of the fire. Coward. You thought Prestes' column was lost. You were scared of prison, of torture, of execution.

FILINTO	I was never a coward. I was never short of bravery.
OLGA	Because you could pick fights. With the men of your troop behind you.
FILINTO	I was a Major. I was decorated for my strength. Commitment. Strategy. Perseverance.
OLGA	And deserted. You even ordered your men to run off across the border, to follow you to Argentina and betray Prestes' cause.
FILINTO	That cause was lost. Fighting had become pointless. They had the upper hand. And were infinitely stronger than us.
OLGA	Is that why you took the money? Stole a hundred million Reales from the column? That belonged to all the men, you grabbed it so you could drink it away with whores, you traitorous pig? Are they the same hundred million Reales you put on Prestes' head, as a personal reward? You caught him anyway, without any reward. You couldn't even buy your revenge.
FILINTO	I'm on the side of the strong, yes, I fight for the side of power, the side of the law. The weak have no right to exist. Only the strong-willed will prevail. I'll never be one of the weak again. A man must know where he belongs.
OLGA	You have no will, Filinto Müller. You're a coward. A cruel little opportunist, a piece of filth. I spit on you. A liar who's lying to himself.
FILINTO	Is there anything more repulsive than the self-righteous gibberish of the people, always believing they've been conned, puffing out their chests, hammering on them with their fists and shouting their plaintive 'me me me' into the world's face, as if there was only the one truth, which belongs to those at the bottom, who have to stamp and kick lying on their backs in order not to be trampled down or simply swept away, as if weakness, despair and protest were the only truths, and not strength

and power and money. Where there is power and influence, there's truth too, a larger truth and more of it and better than that of the oppressed.

I'm not who you take me for. I could have you killed, Olga Benario. It would just take a click of my fingers. Would you like that, a quick end? But I want you to be alright. I am going to help you, you and the child in your belly, which will be a Brazilian, albeit a Jewish one. I can let you give birth to the child here. Let it be issued with a Brazilian passport. You are its mother. You will be able to stay here. The Gestapo will have to forget about you. Prestes will forget about you, because all he will ever see is prison. I'm going to do it. I'm going to save your life. *(He laughs.)* For my own pleasure. For my pleasure. *(He laughs.)* My pleasure.

Blackout.

The ticking of a clock.

MONOLOGUE III

Then Ana arrives. It's night. The lights are on.
She's young and beautiful. Even in this light that's
the yellow of urine she's young and beautiful. Her
name is Ana Libre. I expect nothing of her. She
is determined. How she hates me. I envy her this
hatred. She is the truth and I am the lie, so simple.
I want to be determined. I am still unafraid. The
cell is so narrow. I can feel the child in my belly
and I want to lose it. Lose it. I will kill it. Attain
freedom. Alone. Kill. Kill. Kill. Pull yourself
together, Olga, idiot mother. My child will utter its
first cry in a cell. So. If you're sure of what you're
doing, you'll survive. But how sure can you be of
what you're doing? Are there traitors amongst us?
Show yourselves! Bring the truth to light, even if
it's so dim, one dirty bulb, like this one, you can
easily reach for one thing instead of the other. Then
your fingers stink in the morning because you
accidentally reached into the shitbucket instead
of the rose water. What does it matter, you need
to have conviction.

TRIO I: ACCUSATIO

Two GUARDS bring ANA LIBRE.

GENNY	I've seen you before. This afternoon. When you arrived with the transport.
ANA	–
OLGA	My name's Olga. This is Genny.
GENNY	Hello.
ANA	–
OLGA	That bed there's free. You'd best keep your things in your bag. We've got no cupboard.
GENNY	Yes, we've not got a cupboard.
OLGA	Sit down.
GENNY	Yes, sit down.

ANA swings her bag to the floor, starts rooting around in her things.

GENNY	Aren't you an actress? I think I've seen you, together with that singer… What's his name again? Eugenio?
OLGA	They didn't tell us we were getting someone new.
GENNY	Yes, we don't know anything. But they don't often say anything beforehand.
ANA	–
OLGA	It'll be a bit cramped but we'll manage.
GENNY	We'll get on with each other.
ANA	–
OLGA	Have they interrogated you yet? What are you in for?
GENNY	Are you a political too? I'm in for – 'subversion'.
ANA	Shut your filthy mouth, Olga Benario! You know perfectly well.
OLGA	Me? How am I supposed to know?
ANA	Olga Benario! *(She spits in OLGA's face.)*

GENNY	What are you doing? Are you insane? What's got into you?
ANA	Are you her arse-licker, then?
OLGA	Who are you?
ANA	Who am I? Who am I? I'm going to make your life hell, you filthy traitor. You won't have given them my name for nothing, you miserable piece of filth.
GENNY	What's the matter?
OLGA	What are you saying? That I – denounced you? Who says that?
ANA	Who do you think? Who is the biggest bastard hangman here, that big, thick German Müllerrr.
GENNY	Olga would never do a thing like that, she would never give anyone up to Filinto.
ANA	Be quiet, you echo. *(To OLGA.)* You think you're so superior because you fucked Prestes and the people think you're a hero, you make me throw up, but now you're so small, because they've got you, the good life is over, you viper.
OLGA	It wasn't me. This is one of Müller's games.
ANA	Why should I believe you? What reason would Filinto have to lie to me? He's a pig but this lie makes no sense. Someone snitched on me, why wouldn't it be you?
GENNY	It wasn't Olga, I know her, she's not a traitor.
ANA	If you won't be quiet, you toad, I'm going to shut your mouth for you.
OLGA	Has he interrogated you?
ANA	Why should he, he already knows everything.
OLGA	What did you do?
ANA	What do you want to hear? Should I repeat what you told him?
GENNY	What did you do? What?

ANA	I threw a stinkbomb into the dictator's bedroom.
GENNY	Is that true?
OLGA	That's good. You don't trust me and I don't trust you. We keep watching each other and gradually wear ourselves out. Nice for Filinto. So much easier for him, when he starts the interrogations.
ANA	And you think you're going to catch me out with that trick? I believe you and start chatting. So that's how you get your information. How many prisoners have they already put in with you in this cell?
OLGA	Don't underestimate Filinto. If you start thinking, he'll already be two steps ahead of you. Watch yourself. And when he has you fetched for interrogation, trust only yourself.
GENNY	I… I'm afraid of interrogation. Torture.
ANA	I don't need your advice. You won't hear anything more from me. Let's make small talk. No burnt tongues.
OLGA	Traitor…me. Not a word of it's true.
ANA	Lights out!

Blackout.

A clock ticking.

MONOLOGUE IV

The only way not to be a heroine, a martyr, a victim, is to make myself an accomplice, a collaborator. I myself torture. Torture everyone who crosses my path. Ultimately myself. Myself included. Starting with Luis Prestes I finally end up with me. I torture my brain to death. The way out into emptiness. Forgetting. Having no memory. I remember nothing. What I knew then has gone. Escaped through the convolutions of my brain. Vanished. My head is now a delicate arrangement of bony plates. My head is then smashed. Past life remains in the fragments of bone until the wind tears it away. It spins around, a brain gut, from which it farts out into the world, wet, shriveled skin, lying in a corner of the world, decaying slowly, mould in the wrinkles, musty. That was you, *Olga*, says Filinto, his legs spread above me.

PAS DE DIABLE II

OLGA
I'm a traitor. *(Pause.)* A traitor like you.

FILINTO
I knew it before I even met you.

OLGA
I didn't know I could be such a thing. You made me into one. Ana Libre believes you, even though she knows you're a liar.

FILINTO
The truth is a devil's mask. Every creature goes out of its way.

OLGA
I want an interrogation. An interrogation right down to the final scream.

FILINTO
I've spared you this far. Trivialities, exercises for beginners. Do you really imagine you can fend me off? If you insist on finding out more…

OLGA
No. I'm not a victim. I can help you. I want to help you. I will walk through the corridors of the prison and see people who I will interrogate. I will walk through the streets of the city and see human bodies and human minds which I shall penetrate. Me. I shall be a perpetrator.

FILINTO
Good. You will make a statement. You will name names. I shall bring them to you, the heads with those names. They will stand before you and you will look at them and point to them and say: yes, him and her and him and her and her. And then I will get them to talk – like you.

OLGA
No. No. I'll do it. You'll tell me what I have to do. I will do everything exactly as you wish, but let me do it. You'll show me how. You will induct me in cruelties and tortures. I will learn from you. I will not be a victim. I won't tolerate pain, I will inflict it. I will be feared and despised.

FILINTO
You'll have to stay where you are, Benario. People can't turn themselves into interrogators, they are made into them. It's not a game where you can keep changing your side of the board and the colour of your pieces as often as you like. I have fought for where I am now. Nothing was given to

me. I didn't choose what I've become, I was only ever searching.

OLGA You're right. It's not a game. I'm serious. I'm going to follow you. I will take your place. *(Pause.)* You're standing there, there's a person sitting in front of you. Is he blindfolded? No, he's looking at you. The room is large and wide. You need space. The clock on the wall is covered in broad tape. You've got a lot of time. That person will begin to scream, when that will happen is unclear, but that it will happen is certain. Fear is already etched on his forehead. He's still trying to be calm, proud and defiant, although his wrists are shaking. How will you begin?

FILINTO To begin with – I need the smell of their bodies. I think it's beautiful. Warm, steaming, shorn animals, whose skin is soft and pliant, taking strong breaths. I want to feel their proximity, I want to feel their skin, the pattern of their pores under my fingertips, like honeycomb. Sometimes I stroke them and I can feel the thin, cool film of sweat that's meant to protect the cells. Then I strike. They mustn't begin to stink. If they're afraid, they start stinking. They're such good human machines underneath. They react immediately. I show them electrode clips, ampere meters, coils of wire and syringes and they begin to stink. Not all of them. Those are the interesting ones, though they make the work harder: the ones who don't react as predicted. They're a challenge. The effortless flow is halted. But a machine is never a match for its operator. I will always trace their fault and repair it. And they will do what I want, me.

OLGA I will pull myself together. I will be quite calm. Concentrate on my work. It is work. Knowing that what I do is right. The other person opposite me a hindrance. Hindrances must be removed. Think of something else, something simple. Went hunting and shot ducks, rabbits, reindeer. Their bodies are also soft and yielding. While I'm gutting it I can still feel the warmth of the dead game. I use a sharp knife to slit open the abdominal wall, the incision starts between the legs and runs right up to the throat. The skin gapes wide open. I grab hold of the innards, pull them out of the body and hurl them away. The legs are still twitching but the heart has stopped beating. It's quite easy. I can do it over and over again. It's just a body. It's soon dead. The blood runs away quickly. How easily it runs. *(Pause.)* You only have to overcome resistance once. One tiny bit of resistance. Prick your finger with a needle and squeeze out a drop of blood. Then you can drag a razor blade slowly across the back of your hand, you can stub out burning cigarette tips with a hiss on your skin, eventually you can touch the electric wire with your bare hands. It's only painful the first time. After that it never hurts again. I reduce the pain by making it stronger.

FILINTO   I don't want to hurt anybody. But once it's started I can't go back, I have to carry on. I take everything away from them, their will, their shame and ultimately their life. Sometimes I wake up in the night because I hear that noise. The noise of when two bones in a joint are twisted against each other, the tendons crunch, cartilage explodes, I pull a bit more, a jolt – the skin rips apart, tendons, fat, the lubricant of the joint dangle from the bare, round ends of the bones. That's the noise, it always happens at night, it creaks and crunches and then it stops. And it's so quiet, it's so quiet. *(Pause.)* Then I lie back on my pillow and carry on sleeping.

OLGA   I'll be a good torturer. Thorough. Considered. Remorseless. Sensitive. Appreciative. Delicious – intoxication. I will get drunk on the victim's screams, which fill the cells to the roof in bloody waves. Screams which bounce from wall to wall, rebounding again and again until the many voices turn into a single scream, a scream, the scream of the tortured man, who dies guilty because he was. *(Pause.)* A world full of perpetrators, a world which breaks with the tabu of pain: we get used to the normality of torture early. It is neither forbidden, nor an offence to fight, to rape, to kill. People's fear of inflicting pain on each other has been taken away. We have no more scruples about hurting each other. On the contrary, instead of a kiss on the mouth, a slap on the cheek shows good manners. You're waiting for me to hit you and I hit you and you scream with pleasure.

FILINTO   It's only a convention. A hypocritical threshold put in place by education. It doesn't really exist. *(He laughs.)*

OLGA   And what about your wife? Your children? You educate your children. Do you get them used to breaking down resistance? Do you tell them what you do to the prisoners at home? How you hang them on the parrot's perch, squeeze out their eyes, pull the nails out of their fingers and toes, shove hot electric wires into their penises and send electric shocks through their limbs? Make them familiar with your methods, so they won't be shocked by their father later on and they know what they're capable of. Prepare them thoroughly for torture!

FILINTO   My family is none of your fucking business. I love my family. My wife loves me, she loves and respects me, she's even proud of me, and to my children I'm like a saint.

OLGA   How do you explain your pleasure to them? Your pleasure in doing what you do? Is it what a doctor feels performing a vital operation? Or a carpenter, practicing his craft the way he's been trained? Or – the pleasure of the fear of death, that stinks of blood, pus and rotten flesh?

FILINTO	I love my children. I love and respect my wife. I would never do anything to harm them. Not them. I didn't feel anything. I didn't do anything.
OLGA	*(Alert.)* What happened? What did you do? Did you torture your wife?
FILINTO	No, it's not true, and if it did happen to me, then I did it by mistake, it wasn't intentional, not because I wanted to, it was a mistake, an accident, I didn't want to, she could have defended herself, after all she is my wife.
OLGA	What did you do? How did it happen?
FILINTO	She…was sitting on a chair. At home. Like you are now.
OLGA	You – tied her up?
FILINTO	I only put a rope round her body. It was so easy, as easy as it always is. It happened to me. I didn't know I was at home.
OLGA	Then what? What did you do to her? You injured her?
FILINTO	Yes, yes, I injured her. I pulled my knife out of the inside pocket of my jacket and flicked it open. Like this. She stared at the blade and stammered. I couldn't hear her, I could only see her lips moving. I could only see my knife, my tool, this blade and her face, the body of a woman. It was like it always is. It was like now. It was a stranger I had before me and who I had to get to talk. She screamed. I didn't know her voice. I had to get her to confess. At first I thought she was weak. I only needed to hold on to her and she would tell me everything. But she said nothing. If only she would talk, I'd let go of her.
OLGA	You did untie her, remember. She screamed your name: Filinto. It was your wife. The children were watching, they shouted: Father. You recognized them, remember.

FILINTO	No, I didn't recognize them. I had my knife in my hand, with the sharp blade, walking round and round this screaming, whimpering woman. I punched her in the face a couple of times to get her to stop her sickening noise. I looked at her and she was a stranger. A strange woman. Who was this woman? I didn't know. I only knew what I had to do. I had a job. I must show no weakness. My assistants are waiting for my signal, they're waiting for me to tell them what it is they have to do.
OLGA	You love your wife. You could never do anything to harm her. You didn't do it, Filinto. It was just a dream. It was one of your nightmares. An invention of your brain.
FILINTO	She begged me. I got angry. I'm not weak, not a coward. I won't let myself soften. I took my knife and gave her two quick slices diagonally across the chest, one two, a cross on her chest that she will wear so that she knows she must talk when I want her to. Blood started seeping out of the wounds. I removed her ropes, she was dumb now, I made quick cuts everywhere that her body was bound by the rope. Blood dripped out of her skin. She toppled over and lay on the floor. She held her hands over her cut breasts. Then I recognized her. It was my wife. The children whimpered. – It's Olga.

Blackout.

The ticking of a clock. Turning into a heartbeat.

MONOLOGUE V

The contradiction in torture that is torture: you must know Nothing, remember that Nothing happened. Forget what was. They've got to believe you know Nothing – but you know Everything, you've got to preserve your thoughts, your memories, your knowledge in order to stay yourself. In other words: at the same time you have to forget and retain a perfect memory. You have to shield your torturer from your ultra-memory, your hyper-recall, by *performing* the mindless purely present, the empty past every single moment.

Torture is: finding an unspoken word, an unspoken sentence for every word, every sentence you speak. Yes, for every syllable you think you need to find another you didn't think, you didn't even sense, which is almost the true one. Truth and invention can never be balanced. For every story there is another one. The truth is constantly sabotaged by fantasy, by the imagination. The truth is imagination.

Confront every false sentence with a true one, take one for the other, turn the false one into the true one, true sentences, true people. Under torture false people are made into true people. In the end people die of their truth. Because it is true, because they were, because they are human.

PAS DE DIABLE III

Two GUARDS bring ANA to FILINTO. They remain standing by the door.

FILINTO   Good morning, Ana Libre, my beauty. *(Pause.)*
                   My morning beauty. Today is makeover day,
                   pampering day. *(He laughs.)* I've heard you want
                   to complain about there being so many of you
                   in such a small cell. *(Pause.)* Fleas… Bedbugs…
                   Rats… And the cockroaches make such a row
                   at night. Schrappschrappschrapp. *(He imitates the
                   gnawing noise.)* Disgusting. Nasty. You poor things.
                   Poor poor poor girls. *(He laughs.)* I bet you've all
                   got loads of lice, full of parasites, spiders that spin
                   their sticky webs in your hair, fleas that build their
                   nests inside your pubic hair, where they stay and
                   breed and the little hover flies that nest in your
                   armpits. *(Pause.)* You're like a little dog with tiny
                   little creatures crawling around and breeding in
                   its fur, you're a landlady for hungry layabouts
                   till one day you're empty, sucked dead, you'll be
                   thrown in boiling water, skinned, end up in the
                   stewpot…yum, dog meat, sweet and sour…you
                   little delicacy… *(He laughs.)* But we don't want that,
                   for a start we don't want such a distasteful shaggy
                   louse crawling through the corridors, do we? Let
                   me get rid of the parasites' nests. I'll make you
                   beautiful. *(To the GUARDS.)* My patient here would
                   like some grooming.

*The GUARDS start to undress ANA, who resists strongly. They replace her
clothes, covering her with a hairdresser's apron which doesn't quite
come down to her knees. It is plastic and see-through, but scratched, and
stained in several places, you can see she is not the first person to wear it.
FILINTO puts on a grey hairdresser's overall, which he gets the GUARDS to
button up for him at the back. They go and stand next to the door again.*

FILINTO   *(Points to a chair, to ANA.)* Sit down.

*ANA pushes the chair away. The GUARDS pick it back up again at FILINTO's
signal.*

FILINTO   Make yourself comfortable. *(He laughs.)*

ANA kicks the chair. The GUARDS pick it up and remain standing next to ANA. FILINTO bangs the seat of the chair with the flat of his hand. ANA looks at the GUARDS next to her and sits down. The GUARDS go back to the door. FILINTO has them pass him a pair of scissors. They are serrated. He tests their sharpness: he pulls out one of his hairs and cuts in pieces in the air with satisfaction. He laughs, circles ANA with the scissors and caresses her with their tips, strokes them over ANA's head, nose, mouth, shoulders, neck, arms, breasts etc.

FILINTO   Ana Libre, morning beauty, you've still got a boyfriend, haven't you? Tall, slim, strong. *(Pause.)* He's often collected you from the theatre after the performance. Met you there, huh? Came to watch the show and saw you… Juliet, Ophelia. … Antigone… *(He laughs. Pause.)* Tell me his name, Juliet. *(He laughs.)* His name's Eugenio, isn't it? *(He laughs.)* He wrote leaflets. Nasty, evil leaflets. Manifestos against the government, seditious; inciting the people with his speeches, people you've drummed up furtively, in neighborhood bars, back rooms of restaurants and nights on the beach. Tell me where he is now, who your friends are and accomplices, trust me with this… *(Pause.)* I'm your boyfriend now, Eugenio… I'm your friend…

ANA begins to sing, her voice full of fear. FILINTO is given a pair of plastic gloves by the GUARDS, of the kind used to dye hair; he takes pleasure in pulling them slowly over each individual finger.

ANA   And in the evening he'll go home
And he'll never see me again.
We only knew each other a little
and maybe he loves me after all.

FILINTO   I'm your boyfriend –

ANA   But one day he'll find my red ribbon
on the ground outside the door.
But one day he'll see the writing on the wall:
where did they all disappear to.

FILINTO   I'm your boyfriend –

ANA We only knew each other a little
and maybe he loves me after all
and one day I'll go home
and one day I'll see him again.

*With her last words, FILINTO gathers up her hair and starts cutting it off
with the serrated scissors. Laughing.*

Blackout.

Heartbeat.

What will you say about me afterwards? That I was
your lover? That I was useful? That I was cold?
That we couldn't stand each other? That it was
torture, this forced life as a couple? That we wanted
to leave but were too cowardly to do so? What are
you going to tell them about our child? An accident
of love. They think it was a great, powerful love.
You, Luis Carlos Prestes, and me, Olga Benario.
What do they know? What can they cope with?
We were alone for a long time. Lived in hiding,
the two of us. Like on islands? What would you
take with you to a desert island? *(Pause.)* A man.
No, let me try again, give myself time to think.
(Pause. She laughs.) Two men. So I could stick them
between my legs in turns. *(She laughs.)* I didn't get
the choice. I took what was there. Cool cool cool
you always complained I was cool. Maybe I was
like that, maybe I am like that. Maybe I was just
afraid. But am I going to throw myself immediately
at anything in trousers? Would it have done any
good if I'd loved you? Even when you were alive
they were already constructing your myth, and
me? I was suddenly the sexy lover of Luis Prestes,
knight in shining armour, who had a child with him
without looking. She didn't want it. She was the
one it happened to, not him. Is that supposed to be
my contribution to world revolution? I had a job
to do for the party, which happened to coincide
with my beliefs and was not entirely irreconcilable
with my human inclinations. Perhaps I did love
you. Then that makes me the – just about – living
proof of everything a woman can do these days. A
husband, a child, a career – perhaps even fame, it's
all possible. So I'm a figure of hope. I shall embody
the future for all girls, women, mothers. That is my
part in this game. When biographies are written
about me, I shall be beautiful and clever and brave
and incisive and courageous and always keep my
back up straight. They will be the best evidence

that there are no female intellectuals. They let their brains be cut off along with their hair. My story is: I am going to be gassed. For my beliefs. That is what my child is going to be told.

So that it will emulate me. All children should emulate me. And become like me. Then they will all have firm beliefs and be gassed for their beliefs. The ones who gas them, in the end, when they've got nothing left to do, no more enemies they can gas, die out from boredom. Then the world will be empty. Then I will have succeeded in abolishing humanity. Me, the myth, from which the world has lived.

(She laughs.) You're right. I was cool. I rarely laughed. My beauty was well painted, my ugliness perfectly covered over. I always used mouthwash to cover the bad smell and my brain wasn't the size of a pea. *(Pause.)* Love? *(She laughs out loud.)*

DUET II: NEGATIO

OLGA

Genny Genny Genny. I take your head in my hands, I stroke you, your body lies pressed against mine, Genny. I tell you stories all the time Ana is gone, all the time that the time is stuck, all the time that we're alone. Pay attention.

GENNY

Like my mother? To calm me down?

OLGA

Like a mother. At night, in a storm, to drive away fear. Listen, a story from the interior, from the country's insides, where there's nothing but forest and hills and water and occasionally a couple of houses.

GENNY

Where exactly?

OLGA

In Minas. We lived for a while in Minas Gerais, Luis and I.

GENNY

In the town, in a hiding place.

OLGA

In the country, in the interior. A new beginning. We rented a little sitio. A gorgeous house. It had a stone floor, reddish, square, cut flags, which took on a different colour for each type of daylight. In front of the house there was a veranda of wooden planks. Whenever it rained, the clay soil would soften and give way under your shoes, you had to take them off and leave them until you could scratch the crusts of dried clay off the leather. In the middle of the day the dogs would lie on the veranda in front of the door. If a stranger approached, they'd jump up growling and rush at him, two shaggy devils. Luis was the only one who could keep them quiet. When he put his shoes on and took his gun, they would dash down the path that led to the river and wait for a piece of game to fall in front of their noses.

GENNY

The house was small, tiny. You could hardly move. Slept on the floor.

OLGA

The house had three rooms. At twilight we watched from our hammocks as trails of ants cut a path through the room. Once there was an invasion of red flying ants. They came in through one of the ground floor windows, marched to the corner where the cooking was being done, into a bowl full of Goiaba-Mus, out the other side again, finally up the wall and past the parrot's perch which almost drove poor Rosita mad. She croaked 'dieanimaldie' until she was hoarse, then she gave up and fled into the acacia in front of the house. *(Pause.)* A ceiling of planks had been put up in the main room: there was a ladder leading up to it. That was where we slept.

GENNY   You were sought, persecuted, watched. Filinto was on your trail. No place was safe, no time was quiet, no thought finished –

OLGA   Once we were attacked in our sleep. We'd left the doors and windows open. The robbers came at night and took what they could find in the sala: clay crockery, a sack of dried bananas, a radio. They were nordestinos on the way South, hungry tramps, the people we were fighting for.

GENNY   You had no space. You couldn't move. Because people were after you, looking for your faces, no one was allowed to see you, to recognize you. Food was brought to you, secretly, you could only go out at night, never sleeping, being watchful all the time –

OLGA   In a wide circle around the house was a banana plantation which we didn't maintain. We had no running water in the house and had to fetch it in buckets from the rivers which watered the plantation –

GENNY   That's not true –

OLGA   I got bruises on my shoulders from the weight of the pole –

GENNY   What you're saying isn't true.

OLGA	Luis built a shower a short way from the house: two long bamboo poles, hollowed out and jammed together to divert the water from a little stream –
GENNY	I know different I know better –
OLGA	I stood there for a long time under the stone wall which supported the end of the tube and heard the water run over my body –
GENNY	Lies lies.
OLGA	It spoke to me, when it touched the back of my neck, flowed around my throat, over my shoulders, over my breasts, trickled into my bellybutton, sprayed over elbows, thighs and knees –
GENNY	All lies, lies, les. Be quiet. Will you stop talking. I don't want to hear any more of these fairy tales. That's enough. I'm not your child that you have to sing to sleep.
OLGA	You, you ought to listen to me when I've got something to tell you; do you think I'm just talking here for my own pleasure, you weak little sparrow heart, what do you know, you whimper in the night and grind your teeth while I bite my lips bloody trying to find something that I can tell you to make you stop crying, so you can start to become a human being, a woman who can stand being looked at; but you can't, you fragile thing that's hanging on to my skirts, putting the corner of a blanket in your mouth instead of taking a man, you stupid, disgusting, whinging child –
GENNY	No, I don't want to hear you any more, be quiet, who are you to think you can make me brave, I don't want to hear any more of your stories, all made up, lies the lot of them; you're no better, no different from all of us, I don't want to become like you; I don't want to have to die, I'm afraid, I'm afraid and you, you pretend, you talk, Olga, and I don't believe a word, you never existed, you and

	your Luis, so why did they arrest us, why have I got to be here, why –
OLGA	Alright. Alright. I'll tell you what it was like. Listen to me, one more time, no, you're not a child any more, you can hear the truth. Be calm and listen to me: for almost a year everything was fine. A house in the city in Rio. Light. Roomy. Friends. We could go out, if we were careful. Then underground. Hiding in a tiny dark stuffy safehouse. For months. Without ever being allowed on the street. Don't see anyone. Doors and windows shut so no passer by can hear our voices. In the darkened room we only make light to stop people seeing our shadows. I often didn't know if it was day or night, and I used to wake up out of dreams because I thought I was suffocating –
GENNY	No spring, no river close by where you could fetch water, bruises on your shoulders from the weight of the pole….
OLGA	At night we could walk around a small courtyard with a wall as tall as a man; we wore ponchos and straw hats because we were afraid the neighbours might recognize our sex and faces, we'd walk around there at night in circles, at night… A comrade came once a week and brought us bread and cheese and milk. The rest of the time we lived out of tins. He also brought newspapers which often had Luis's name in them and the description of an unknown woman.
GENNY	A beautiful house. A new beginning. A stone floor, reddish flags, a veranda made of wooden planks. Dogs by the door. Hunting along the river. *(She laughs out loud.)* That's how you think yourself through.
OLGA	We were so afraid that they'd find us. We didn't know how long we could hold out. Then the comrade didn't come any more and we knew that

they had got him. At night we listened to every step and by day we flinched every time a child cried.

GENNY

Attacked while you slept. Windows and door open. Stories of robbers. *(She laughs.)* They took what they could find: clay crockery, bananas, a radio. Nordestinos heading south, hungry, not sleeping… the people we were fighting for. *(She laughs loudly.)*

OLGA

It took fourteen days. One day they beat the door down. We tore open a window and tried to escape but there were soldiers with machine guns ready to fire in every street, uniforms in every garden and on all the rooves. They'd been combing the city for weeks. *(She laughs.)* They took Luis still in his pyjamas…and barefoot…and I shouted 'Don't shoot for God's sake don't shoot…' and they led him like that, as he was, through the street, two machine guns behind him, one on either side of him, them in their uniforms with their heavy boots and Luis barefoot…in pyjamas, with his hands up.

Blackout.
Heartbeat.

My heart is a cage. But you planted the seed for your brood in my lap, Luis Prestes. The bird is growing in my belly. Soon it will hatch out, the little chosen one, the cheeky little beast. It will stay in prison. It will always stay in prison.

We should talk. He wants to get us to talk. He wants to get us to be silent. Anyone who's dumb goes mad. If you ever get to live, I'll tell you. You'll never get to meet our neighbour in the cells. He's a Lieutenant in the Air Force. He grants me a wish. Once. Secretly. Exercising in the yard. He draws the air force's planes for me, draws them with a grey pencil stub on scraps of paper. Do you know what I do with them? Your mother looks after you. Fighters, dive bombers, light and heavy bombers, strike aircraft: daytime and night fighters, and in between the tiny parachutists, there were some pretty pictures. Genny unpicks an old blanket; with the thread she embroiders the fighters, dive bombers, light and heavy bombers, strike aircraft and parachutists on to your little dungarees and shirts. Genny can do embroidery. We put a couple of lines up in our cell, diagonally across the cell. Like this. From one wall to the other. Over our beds. And hang the little dungarees and shirts and trousers up on them. Our cell is full of children's toys, war toys. In our cell the air force dangles from the line just waiting to be worn. You'll look pretty in them. Just like the smart clean little children who are taken for walks in the park holding their nanny's hand. On Sundays. They're allowed out then.

TRIO II: DEMENTIA

Two GUARDS bring ANA back into the cell. Her hair is short as a matchstick, as if it has been eaten off. She wears the same clothes as before the hair cut, but some of them are worn the wrong way round, with buttons done up the wrong way, etc. ANA is disturbed and hardly takes any notice of her surroundings. GENNY screams.

OLGA	*(Quietly.)* Ana. *(Pause.)* What…what have they done to you… *(Pause.)* Ana, what the Devil have they done to you?
GENNY	Ana… *(Pause.)* Oh my God oh my God Holy Mary mother of God.
OLGA	*(Touches ANA cautiously.)* Ana…love…
ANA	*(Restless.)* Eugenio… Eugenio…
OLGA	What's she saying?
GENNY	Her boyfriend.
OLGA	*(Attempts again to stroke ANA.)* Ana, my love, love…
ANA	Eugenio, go away, go away, I don't want to see you again, go away, you're hurting me…no…
OLGA	Yes…yes…it's me, I'm Eugenio, I'm your boyfriend, I'm with you, come on, hold my hand, trust me, it's me, I'm your boyfriend…
ANA	Noooo… Go away, leave me alone, get out… I don't love you any more, you make me, won't let me, leave me alone, please, leave me alone…no…

GENNY and OLGA understand. OLGA lets go of ANA.

GENNY	Filinto!
OLGA	I ought to kill him.
GENNY	Yes, we should, and tomorrow instead of him, another one or two or three or a whole gang of them.
OLGA	Then take a sharp knife and cut our veins, mine first and then yours, so that there's lots of blood once and for all and he can drink himself to death on it.

ANA   Red red

Lighting up outside the door.

> I've lost my hairband
> I can't find it
> I've lost my dearest love
> I can't find him
>
> Red red
> lighting up outside the door
> if he finds it
> he's mine
>
> *She laughs.*

Blackout.

Heartbeat.

MONOLOGUE VIII

I was so badly prepared for the day when it did arrive. I didn't think I could still defend myself. I would have let it happen, without any resistance. My child will be born in Germany. They came to fetch me and take me to the ship. The ship with the swastika is at the docks and is waiting for me, to go with me to Germany. I'm allowed a sea voyage. But my fellow prisoners want to prevent this. They don't want to let me go. From one cell to the next, all the prisoners have a code: when they come to fetch Olga, they'll get a riot. The ship with the swastika flag has been in the harbour since yesterday. Since yesterday we've kept watch and listened for Filinto's footsteps. Finally, long strides all the way down the corridor. One two three one two three. Filinto Müller, his hobnail boots, two three, his henchmen, with reinforced heels each of them. I can already hear the drumming, it starts quietly, reproduces itself with Filinto, following his footsteps – and preceding them. Drumming. Drumming. Tin plates on cell doors, wooden clogs against iron bars, bare fists against the walls, flat hands on the floor, spoons, forks, cups against metal pipes, quiet at first, then louder and louder, faster and faster, louder louder, faster faster, shouts: Get Filinto Müller, everybody shout, get Filinto Müller, get the bastard out, in time, in time, Filinto's already walking quicker, they're driving him, all the cells are on their feet, the guards along the corridors in panic, batter the cells with their truncheons, fetch the dogs, this time there's no point, they scream everything down: Get Filinto Müller, heat the place up with him, Genny's drumming too, drumming like crazy, running from one wall to the other, to the door, to the wall and back, she's hitting everything. She screams, come on Ana, drum, drum, drum, everything depends on how loud you can drum, you've got to drum like a mad woman. Ana understands this. She takes the shit bucket, looks to see if it's empty. She turns it up and says: this is my drum. She climbs up on her bed and starts drumming. She sits stiffly and stares blankly ahead of her. She sees nothing. She too, hears the footsteps getting closer. She drums. Louder, Ana, louder. They can't hear you. Louder. Ana drums louder. She too gets faster and faster. She starts humming. She hums. It's a wild, deep humming. Slowly she opens her mouth and lets a terrible sound be heard. Louder. Louder. She's shouting. She's shouting she's shouting she's shouting she's shouting. I hold my ears closed, press my hands as hard as I can against my ears. The drums. The screams. Now: the footsteps have stopped. He has stood still. The drumming triumphs. He turns around. He goes back. One two three. They both follow him. Two three. The drums celebrate. The cells dance. Music. The drums are music. Finished.

QUARTET

OLGA   They'll manage it the second time. The second time Filinto will be cleverer. He'll not make a mistake. He'll come back when we don't expect it. The ships in the harbour don't fly flags any more. They don't have German names. One of them is going to Germany nevertheless, with a German Captain. I've stopped defending myself.

ANA has an empty food tin in front of her and is busy throwing pebbles into it. For a while all that can be heard is their monotonous clicks.

GENNY   *(Watches ANA for a while, then harshly.)* Tick tick tick, the time is marching wrong, and all we do is march along. *(Pause. To OLGA.)* Wasn't there a promise once? Of a passport? Of right to remain?

OLGA   I'll remember you through the baby things. Both of you. Every time I take something out of the bag and dress the child with it, I'll remember that you sewed it.

Footsteps. FILINTO enters with two medical orderlies.

FILINTO   It's time. I'm having you taken to the hospital. You need to have your examination. It's what you always wanted. So that everything goes smoothly with the birth. *(He laughs.)* Quick march.

GENNY   It's a trap. He won't take you to the hospital. Look at them. Is that what carers look like? You won't be able to defend yourself..

OLGA   They're not going to be kept waiting.

FILINTO   The game's over.

ANA   My boyfriend. *(She laughs.)* Do you see? My boyfriend's come. *(She approaches FILINTO.)* My darling, my darling, dance ring a ring a roses with me, cuddle me, caress me, I am your true love. Don't you recognize me? Don't you recognize me? *(Pause.)* I wish I had a little knife, to sharpen with a stone and when it is as sharp as sharp can be, I'd cut up all your bones.

FILINTO gives the GUARDS a sign to take hold of ANA. OLGA steps in front of them and pulls her away.

OLGA   Ana, come and help me, I want to pack a few things.

ANA   He must die, die he must, ladies, because he looks for the mouth of another, or because he is not the one I think he is? Out of jealousy or necessity. I wish I had a little knife to sharpen with a stone…

OLGA   Here, take this and this. Pack those.

ANA   I was never a child. Why do you want to have a child? There are no parts for children. All soppy.

FILINTO   Stop packing. It's a waste of time. Progress is easier without bagage.

GENNY   She, she's not coming. She's not allowed to go. You're going to kill her.

FILINTO   *(Indicating the orderlies, to GENNY.)* Should they give you an injection to calm you down?

OLGA   It's all right, Genny. – Just a pair of shoes. A blanket for the child. A comb.

FILINTO   Take her away!

GENNY   Olga!

ANA   Mercy me, what's rustling in the corn, it's poor Susie, looking all forlorn… Oh dear, now I've completely forgotten to count all the notes, now I'll just have to go back and start all over again…

Blackout.

Heartbeat.

MONOLOGUE IX

They took me to Hamburg. The ship was called La Coruña. I lay below decks in a little shed and I could hear the men's footsteps above my head. Sometimes I'd be allowed onto the deck at night, like a dog that's allowed to go and piss in a corner and I could see the stars and smell the sea. Cool. The journey took us three weeks. At sea. Just water. Thirst. The sea went like this: unsteady. Everything moved up and down. I puked and puked and had nothing but my hands to wipe away the stinking vomit. The creature in my belly screamed: hunger. We didn't dock at a single port. No one should be able to find me. They were waiting for me on the quay. A Gestapo car, bars on the windows, took me to Berlin. That's where my cell was. A room for me alone. A concrete bed. My belly was a barrel. I lay on the concrete and bore a child Anita. Like that. My child Anita. I had a daughter Anita and I was in prison. I was allowed to keep her in my cell, as long as I could breast feed. That lasted fourteen months. One year and two months. Every day I put her basket in the yard for an hour. Fresh air. The first thing she ever saw: my cell. My walls. That's where she learnt to walk. My cell measured four and a half adult steps by two and a half. How many child steps. She would have been able to spell: O.L.G.A. To decipher the writing on my walls. Anita's gone. My child has gone. They took her away and brought me to the camp. Three years I've been in this concentration camp, three years that she's been with relatives in Paris. Or in Mexico? I don't know. Someone will be looking after her. She's now one two three four five years old and she'll forget her mother.

EXITUS

I am alone.
This is my – room
Extermination facility.
I have arrived.
Bernburg.
I call the place by its name.
I am Olga. I am alone.
This is my empty room.
A – chamber.
I can already smell the gas. They say it doesn't
smell.
But that's not true.
I will breathe it in deeply. My lungs fill
up the last times with Zyklon-B-Gas.
It's the sea and the almond trees that I breathe.
I have so looked forward to the sea
How good the air is here so fresh
not stuffy like it is at home
in my cell
I'm blooming
I feel dizzy
clean air gives you
red cheeks
I'm feeling light
my throat itches

I open my eyes wide the wide wide country
My heart beats quietly
lightly I keep on living
I breathe one more time

Blackout.

INNOCENCE

This translation of *Innocence* was commissioned by the Goethe Institut and first produced in the UK by Arcola Theatre in association with KP Productions on 6th January 2010 with the following cast:

ELISIO	Okezie Morro
FADOUL	Nathaniel Martello-White
FRAU HABERSATT	Ellen Sheean
WIFE	Miranda Cook
HUSBAND	Alexander Gilmour
FRAU ZUCKER	Ann Mitchell
ROSA	Caroline Kilpatrick
FRANZ	Chris Hannon
ELLA	Maggie Steed
HELMUT	Michael Fitzgerald
ABSOLUTE	Meredith MacNeill
YOUNG DOCTOR	Alexander Gilmour

Director	Helena Kaut-Howson
Designer	Lara Booth
Lighting and Video Designer	Alex Ward
Sound Design	Mark Thurston

Characters

ELISIO

black illegal immigrant

FADOUL

black illegal immigrant

ABSOLUTE

a young blind woman

FRAU HABERSATT

a woman on her own

FRANZ

a carer for the deceased

ROSA

his wife

FRAU ZUCKER

her mother

ELLA

an ageing philosopher

HELMUT

her husband, a goldsmith (non-speaking)

THE PRESIDENT

Parents of a girl who has been killed (Scene 2)

Two suicides (6)

Chorus of survivors of the attack (7)

A young doctor (11)

Chorus of motorists (14)

If ELISIO and FADOUL are cast with black actors then please do
so because they are good actors and not for the sake of some
sort of forced authenticity, which is not necessary. Otherwise,
no blacking up, artificial theatrical devices such as masks etc.
are preferred.

Music:

Optional for the end of scene 1: Sandy Dillon, *Float*.

Optional for the end of scene 8: *Send me a dollar*.

Obligatory for scene 19: *I m just blue*.

THE SEA THAT FILLS THE HORIZON I

FRAU HABERSATT'S CASES I

FRANZ FINDS WORK, FRAU ZUCKER FINDS A
HOME, ROSA FINDS HOPE

ELLA I

FOUND

TO JUMP OR NOT TO JUMP

FRAU HABERSATT'S CASES II

GOD IN A BAG

FRANZ SHOWS HIS WORK, FRAU ZUCKER
SHOWS A SOFT HEART, ROSA SHOWS HER
BODY

ABSOLUTE

JUMPED

ELLA II

FRAU HABERSATT TRIES TO AVOID PROBATION

AND EVERYONE

LIGHT

RECOGNITION

ELLA III

THE UNRELIABLE WORLD

THE SEA THAT FILLS THE HORIZON II

Blood roars in the thermometer.

It is unpleasant to die, sir, when you've nothing to leave behind in life and nothing is possible in death other than what you leave behind you in life!

It is unpleasant to die, sir, when you've nothing to leave behind in life and nothing is possible in death other than what you leave behind you in life!

It is unpleasant to die, sir, when you've nothing to leave behind in life and nothing is possible in death other than what you can leave behind you in life!

César Vallejo, The Windows Shook

1. THE SEA THAT FILLS THE HORIZON I

ELISIO   Two friends are walking by the sea that fills the horizon. Two friends, Fadoul and Elisio. *(Pause.)* At the water's edge they walk up and down, up and down, trying to cast a glimpse into the future.

Pause.

FADOUL   But the future stares back out of angry hollows ringed with charcoal, sockets with no eyes inside, so there's nothing more to be said about later, no afterwards to discuss.

ELISIO   Said Fadoul and was silent. Elisio on the other hand is an optimist by nature. Born in the south of the country. Where the sun is highest. In the blue delta of the Nile. He'd felt the sweetest teats of the fattest mother ewes in his mouth. *(Pause.)* But out of friendship with Fadoul, in order not to offend this self-pitying misery guts, he was silent too.

Silence. ELISIO nudges FADOUL in the ribs.

FADOUL   I'll tell you what I can see. I can see the sky and it could be the sky over the desert; but the sky over the desert is high and clear and wide and lets your thoughts reach right up to the stars. *(Pause.)* I can see a sea of water and I can't recognize my sea of sand anywhere in it, because the sea of sand moves slowly and constantly, so that you can keep pace with it and never lose your way. *(Pause.)*

This sky is low; heavy clouds hang round my head, right over my head, as if they are about to rip it off with the next gust of wind; the sea restless, waves, born incalculably out of the deep, charge at me; then they dance backwards, with their arms outstretched, tempting me away, away… I don't know where.

Silence.

FADOUL   The people in this place are completely mad. Taking off their clothes and swimming, in this cold.

ELISIO	Where.
FADOUL	There – . That woman there – .

A woman with red hair undresses slowly some distance away from the two men. She places her clothes together carefully one after another in a neat pile, as if she is placing them in a cupboard. Her movements are fluid and concentrated. She leaves the pile behind her and goes into the water. She sees no-one.

FADOUL	This sea is not the future you promised me.

Pause.

ELISIO	Because you're blind. Or because you've lost your courage. Looking at this sea is freedom, Fadoul.
FADOUL	Fuck Freedom, I want sand.

Silence.

ELISIO	There was one thing Elisio wanted to avoid, he wanted to avoid seeing his friend Fadoul unhappy. So he was thinking up a rosy new story for both their futures, when – look over there – Fadoul –
FADOUL	What.
ELISIO	There – there's something –
FADOUL	What.
ELISIO	I don't know – the prow of a ship, a rudder – the misty air – it's moving –
FADOUL	Where.
ELISIO	A buoy maybe, in the wind – an oil barrel – can't you hear it –
FADOUL	My ears are full of dirt.
ELISIO	There she's swimming. There's someone swimming there and making signals – . Hello-o –
FADOUL	Be quiet. What are you shouting for –
ELISIO	There's someone swimming out there. That woman, the woman with the red hair.
FADOUL	Do you know her.
ELISIO	No.

FADOUL	What are you shouting for then. She might be the police.
ELISIO	Hello-o – . She's waving to me. *(He starts getting undressed.)* I'm coming –
FADOUL	She's waving, is she? How can you tell, Elisio, at this distance with your eyes, as sharp and tireless as a mole, that this female body is waving to you and is not one of the police?
ELISIO	Hurry up, Fadoul, come on, quick –
FADOUL	She's calling for you, is she? What if I can hear her calling for me, old friend, it's me she's calling to?
ELISIO	*(Almost naked.)* She's calling for help, Fadoul, she's drowning, quick –
FADOUL	Fadoul realises the seriousness of the situation with a single glance. His friend has, as so often, as almost always, been right all along. A woman is drowning while he stands around and talks. What could be more beautiful than saving a human being from drowning. Thousands upon thousands of times in his childhood and then later in his youth, both of which he had spent in the desert, he had imagined what it would be like to save someone from drowning; admittedly this required a lot of imagination, on the other hand it wasn't all that difficult, in his imagination Fadoul coloured in the sea of desert sand that surrounded him blue, he let the rain fall and in his dreams the palm trees became green underwater algae, but while he was immersing himself in all this, there was in the unreal reality he was just dipping his toe into, a woman whose life was evidently in danger, and he remembered that he couldn't swim.
ELISIO	I'll go by myself.
FADOUL	Alright. I'll try it.
ELISIO	Where. Can you still see her.
FADOUL	A hand, there, there's a hand.

ELISIO	Straight ahead. Come on.
FADOUL	And then.
ELISIO	Save her.
FADOUL	We take her to the hospital.
ELISIO	Ye-es.
FADOUL	They take all our particulars.
ELISIO	That doesn't matter now.
FADOUL	It does matter.
ELISIO	We'll take her there, to the hospital, and she can go in.
FADOUL	She won't go in. She's unconscious.
ELISIO	We'll leave her outside the door and ring the bell. *(Pause.)* But she can't say what happened.
FADOUL	They want papers. They arrest us. No papers. And then. *(Pause.)* Perhaps she's illegal too. That would make three of us.
ELISIO	We give a false name and get out.
FADOUL	Quick and clever.
ELISIO	Right.
FADOUL	Right.
	Silence.
FADOUL	Where is she.
ELISIO	Can't see her. Can't see her. Can't see her.
FADOUL	The waves. And that – There – There – There –
ELISIO	What – Where – Hello-oo –
FADOUL	Just foam. Foam, that's all.
ELISIO	Where – Where – Where is she –
FADOUL	Nothing.
	Silence.
FADOUL	Nothing.
	Silence.

ELISIO   You, you mis-born son of a fat coyote bitch,
           you whining windbag, you desert bastard you
           sack of fleas you cretin in sandals you towel-
           headed layabout you palm tree waver you soft
           harem fucker you slimy spawn of oil drillers you
           mendacious mirage –

He grabs FADOUL by the throat. They fight. FADOUL wins. Pause.

FADOUL   Put your clothes back on. *(Pause.)* PUT YOUR
           CLOTHES BACK ON.

*The surface of the sea is empty. Waves hit the shore and retreat from it
again. The beach is naked except for the pile of clothes.*

2. FRAU HABERSATT'S CASES I

FRAU HABERSATT   It lights up the whole street, that motion sensor of
                 yours.

Pause.

                 Can I come in. May I.

Pause.

                 That clock's loud.

WIFE   The woman just walked straight into our hall. And
                 then she walked straight into our living room.
                 She, how can I put it, slid along the walls. And
                 my husband who hadn't said anything followed
                 her with his arms outstretched, like he was trying
                 to catch a chicken or herd it away. But he didn't
                 dare touch her.

FRAU HABERSATT   What a lot of books you've got.

Silence.

                 Feels like being in church.
                 Worshipful.

Pause.

                 All those words shut in. Have you freed them all.
                 Have you read them all.

Pause.

                 My God, you'll think, my God,
                 another of those cheap magazine readers
                 wrong.
                 I would never buy a subscription
                 door to door,
                 it's all a con,
                 you order three, they deliver six,
                 and then it's automatically extended by a year,
                 and there's nothing you can do about it.
                 You must belong to a book club.

It's very hygienic,
the books from the library have such
greasy pages and spots on the cover.

Pause.

My son wrote poems,
you should know that.

Pause.

To you my rose
My love is always true
You my rose
I'll pluck your lovely bloom.

Silence.

Nice, isn't it.

HUSBAND She actually takes a photograph down from the shelf, with her intrusive stranger's hands she takes a silver framed photograph down from the shelf, the last photograph of our daughter. My wife is terrified, she is afraid that the photograph could be damaged in some way and that would be as if our daughter had to die all over again. I want to hold my hands under the frame, but I can't manage it, they stand there in front of my stomach, forming an idiotic little nest.

WIFE My husband is a lumbering goalkeeper, trying in vain to catch a ball from his opponent. He knows he has never trained properly, his reactions are poor, he is short of breath. He knows that he's clumsy and he's going to end up in the mud. He's got no ambition, he has no courage, his body invites derision. It says, sit down, make yourself at home, become part of me. Even derision gets a bit tired of being inside his body, it yawns and looks out for new victims. It moves out and leaves him alone. A shivering shell, a jittery skin. He just accepts it.

FRAU HABERSATT   Oh, I'm sorry.

I haven't introduced myself.

WIFE   She sits down. She lets her handbag drop down next to the armchair as if she's never going to get up again.

FRAU HABERSATT   My name is Habersatt.

I'm Udo's mother.

Silence.

HUSBAND   After a short never-ending silence my wife has fallen into a prolonged state of catalepsy and I don't know how I'm going to get *her* out of our house. So I just close my eyes for a while.

Quiet.

FRAU HABERSATT   That's a nice cross you've got up there on the wall.

Silence.

FRAU HABERSATT   Forgiveness.

Forgive us for existing.

And ever coming near you.

And turning your lives into purgatory.

That's why I'm here.

I'm asking your forgiveness.

Pause.

Forgiveness for being born.

For giving birth to a son.

Forgiveness for what he did to your daughter –

Don't be afraid, I won't say it out loud.

Pause.

You probably know more than I do.

Pause.

I know, I know,

that the only true forgiveness can come from God.

But I promise,

if you can make a start,

that would comfort our suffering a great deal.

Silence.

WIFE   We –

               Your –

HUSBAND   I keep calm.

WIFE   This is monstrous, it's –

               it's monstrous –

HUSBAND   *(To his wife.)* Calm down – calm down –

               I'm keeping calm. I'm keeping calm. Calm now.

FRAU HABERSATT Yes, I am asking a lot,

               how much,

               too much perhaps.

               All I want –

Pause.

               I used to be a secretary once

               in a printer's.

               The smell of damp, of freshly printed paper –

               They printed everything,

               brochures, posters, political periodicals,

               and these little, these little porn mags

               too,

               only no books.

               The smell of damp, freshly –

Pause.

               All I want

               is just

               a chance.

Pause.

               Your forgiveness won't help

               my son very much.

He will be sentenced
and have to stand before God his judge.

Pause.

But I,
I'm on my own.

Silence.

I always told him,
those stains won't come out at sixty degrees.
He was left-handed –
always spilt everything with his right.
I forced him to do it that way,
you understand.
It wasn't evil of me.
But the stab wounds were left-handed,
I know, left-handed,
and with such power,
with such power –

Pause.

I'm wasting my time here.
You don't understand me.

WIFE   *(To her husband.)* I can't stand – *(Chokes.)*

HUSBAND   My dear, dear Frau Habersatt – my wife, I
can see, is going to have to be sick, she's been
sick every night, since we've known how our
daughter – instead of going to sleep, she throws
up into a toilet a couple of times and sometimes
she misses. My dear, dear Frau Habersatt, you
don't need to feel guilty and there's no need for
you to apologize. You don't have to stare at the
cross, we used to be Christians, but our belief
has not helped us, it has finished us; the cross is a
mocking reminder of more peaceful days. Please
go and see your confessor; we didn't bring our
child up to be a perpetrator, we didn't understand

our responsibilities; we brought our child up to be a victim, helpful, friendly and trusting, always ready to give and to listen and to sympathise, and don't tell us again that there's nothing you can do about it, because we, we can't do anything about it either, we're members of a society which believes in resolving conflict through negotiation, we were all taught that conscientiously as a sort of punishment for the war, and now will you please leave and please forgive me for screaming –

Pause.

That's what I wanted to tell her, but I didn't actually do it, just in my head. What I actually did was offer her a cup of tea, I sat down on the arm of her chair, held her moist hand and surrounded her with my concern while my wife had collapsed under the table, whimpering, crying into her vomit and when it got dark, I clicked on the lamp and asked: dear Frau Habersatt, might I be able to give you a lift home? Or would you prefer to spend the night in our spare room, then you won't be so alone?

3. FRANZ FINDS A JOB , FRAU ZUCKER FINDS A HOME, ROSA FINDS HOPE

Rosa and Franz's home. Just one room, only the essentials. A table which is also a bed or a bed which is also a table. A television with the permanent image of the President, alternately either distorted or quartered by interference.

ROSA and her mother, FRAU ZUCKER, who has a bandaged foot and walks on crutches. ROSA has red hair and resembles the woman who drowned in Scene 1.

    Silence.

FRAU ZUCKER	*(Smokes.)* If I worked in a petrol station –

    Silence.

FRAU ZUCKER	If I worked in a petrol station –
ROSA	Oh, Mum.

    Silence.

FRAU ZUCKER	If I worked in a petrol station, all it would take is one cigarette to blow everything sky high. *(Pause.)* That's what I think sometimes. *(Pause.)* But at home I don't even have gas. Where am I supposed to begin.
ROSA	Oh, Mum.

    Silence.

FRAU ZUCKER	And how are you.
ROSA	Jesus.

    Pause.

FRAU ZUCKER	Still going to the office every day.
ROSA	Nine to five.
FRAU ZUCKER	Still chief sales assistant.
ROSA	Oh, Mum.
FRAU ZUCKER	I rang that mail order company of yours recently. Because of that special offer: a machine to take your blood pressure for 5 euro 95, that really is cheap. *(Pause.)* But you didn't answer the phone.
ROSA	But Mum there are loads of people like me.

FRAU ZUCKER	And you put up with it.

Silence.

FRAU ZUCKER	You don't use your talents –

Silence.

FRAU ZUCKER	If I was your age again, then I wouldn't get diabetes. But the toe's gone and the rest is just a matter of time –
ROSA	But Mum –
FRAU ZUCKER	If I worked in a petrol station –

Enter FRANZ. Looks at the others as if he is about to say something. Then instead stares at the President.

FRAU ZUCKER	Well Franz, still unemployed.
FRANZ	*(To ROSA.)* Hi love.
ROSA	Hi love.

Silence.

FRANZ	Hello, mother in law.

FRANZ sits down in front of the TV, uses the remote like a weapon against the screen. The President remains stubbornly distorted. Pause.

FRAU ZUCKER	So, how long did you have to wait for your number to be called today.

Pause.

FRANZ	Are they all yours, those suitcases outside.
FRAU ZUCKER	See Rosa, I was in the hospital yesterday. A check up. You ought to see it, the toe, or rather the no-toe, the wound's inflamed and is eating its way up here. The doctor says to me, Frau Zucker, he says, your diabetes is in its final phase. Nothing can stop it now. We'll have to amputate your foot at the ankle. I can't inject my own insulin any more, my eyes are so bad; I need looking after. But they'll only take me as an outpatient, because of the insurance. You understand. *(Deep breath. Pause.)*

	And I need people to talk to me. To talk to me. I am human.
ROSA	You're going into a home?
FRAU ZUCKER	You know, I had my dreams. *(Pause.)* For forty years, I dreamt my dreams in the post office, forty years. And I could have gone to university. *(Pause.)* And I had four children, where are they all now. You're the only one I've got left. *(Pause.)* No sign of a father anywhere. *(Pause.)* I was a communist and wanted to do it all by myself.
ROSA	That was a mistake, Mum.
FRAU ZUCKER	You said it, Rosa. You should serve the people, serve them. *(Pause.)* Your husband had the best prospects but he couldn't even last till the physical.
FRANZ	You can't see the surprise I've got.
FRAU ZUCKER	He'd rather be on the dole.

Pause.

FRANZ	Not any more.
ROSA	You're going to start again –
FRAU ZUCKER	Well, congratulations.
FRANZ	*(With suppressed pleasure.)* Yes, yes, not any more.
FRAU ZUCKER	I would have liked to have studied, would have liked that. To have studied something. Don't know what. Law, maybe, I think these are lawyer's hands. These are lawyer's hands, just like Franz there is definitely running round with doctor's hands. Look at them, doctor's hands. I studied law for a term and then stopped. The books were too thick. The sentences were too long. All together a jungle. And not a machete anywhere – or even a clearing.
ROSA	Mum, you never studied law, not ever –
FRAU ZUCKER	I might have done. I might very well have done. *(Pause.)* Or I think it was – archaeology. Yes, that was it. *(Looks at her hands.)* Archaeologist's shovels.

(Pause.) I dug them out, the poems of the human heart, its sadness, its rhymes. *(Silence.)* Endless possibilities, you've got endless possibilities before you.

FRANZ   I'm not going to study any more. My hands, they wanted something else. My thoughts wanted something else. I've found a job.

Pause.

ROSA   Oh Franz, darling, darling Franz, at last we can – I can think about – we could –

FRAU ZUCKER   She stutters around as if she was already pregnant and drunk with hormones. But a child is too expensive for dear Franz, now that I'm going to be living with you.

Silence.

ROSA   You said you were going into a home.

FRAU ZUCKER   That's what you said. I can't afford a home, I'm moving in with you. I'm handing over responsibility for me to you. Reluctantly. *(Silence.)* Yes, that's my surprise.

Silence.

ROSA   Mum, we've only got one room. And one table that we sleep on or one bed that we eat off.

FRAU ZUCKER   A soft mattress and a screen between me and you, that'll be enough. You've got no imagination.

ROSA   I'm at work all day –

FRAU ZUCKER   If Franz is earning you can resign.

FRANZ opens and closes his fists.

FRAU ZUCKER   Forty years I dreamt my dreams in the post office, forty years. I need people to talk to me. I am human.

ROSA   Yes, Mum. You are human.

FRAU ZUCKER   If I worked in a petrol station –

FRANZ opens and closes his fists. FRAU ZUCKER goes to fetch her suitcases, ROSA helps.

FRAU ZUCKER   I don't want a grandchild now, Rosa. You can do that once there's nothing left of me for them to amputate. Then you'll have room enough –. Burn my old heart and conceive a new one. But a child that's just learning to walk and my leg only comes down to here, I'm not doing that –

FRANZ opens and closes his fists.

FRANZ   The burning I can help you with.

FRAU ZUCKER   Franz, you hardly speak – then when you do, I don't understand you.

FRANZ   I start tomorrow at Berger's. Berger & Sons.

ROSA   What's that. A business. A factory. A transport company.

FRANZ   Undertakers. I collect the deceased, wash them, dress them, lay them out, put them in coffins. *(Pause.)* I felt their skin. Life cools very slowly, and a glowing core remains behind.

ROSA   *(Serious.)* That is a beautiful job, Franz. *(Pause.)* That is a beautiful job with a soul. And a big, big responsibility. I'm pleased about that, very pleased.

FRANZ   *(Quiet.)* Rosa, I love you.

ROSA   *(Quiet.)* I love you too.

FRANZ   *(Quiet.)* Now we can have a child.

ROSA   *(Quiet.)* Now we can have a child.

FRAU ZUCKER unpacks her suitcase and organizes a bed for herself.

FRANZ   Do you want any help, Mum.

FRAU ZUCKER   Washing dead bodies.

FRANZ   It's a service.

FRAU ZUCKER   Then I'm in safe hands when the time comes. And what do you earn there.

FRANZ   We'll manage, Mum.

FRAU ZUCKER   Why are you calling me Mum. Not you. *(Pause.)*
                I had an image of mankind and a dream of
                happiness. *(Pause. Switches the President off.)* I wanted
                to liberate people from their ping pong clubs.
                (Pause.) Now I dream from one cigarette to the
                next. But what will you leave behind. Apart from
                your bourgeois domesticity.

FRAU ZUCKER lies down to sleep. Silence.

FRANZ   I wouldn't have been a good doctor. I lack the
                compassion.

ROSA   I know. You look right through me, as if someone
                else was standing behind me. But our child will
                look at you like a mirror. Maybe then you'll find
                peace.

*FRANZ and ROSA lie down to sleep. It goes dark. The drowned woman
with red hair enters quietly. She's naked, a walking corpse, and lies down
between ROSA and FRANZ.*

4. ELLA I

HELMUT, Ella's husband, has a goldsmith's magnifier in his eye and is busy making something very small with his hands. The television shows a speech by the President. ELLA watches with the sound off.

ELLA   I've written the President
how many articles, essays, even
letters to his newspaper
and his TV channel.
Answers to his speeches.
But not sent a single one of them.
Not a single line.
Demonstrating the limits of populism,
dumbing-down,
this voice of the people stuff.
Or
becoming the voice of the people myself.

Pause.

Enlightenment.

Laughs.

I don't want to dirty myself with politics,
in the end;
daily business goes by,
a footnote in history, a corrupt disc in the archive;
daily business dissolves
into the history of great upheavals
yet to come.

Pause.

But who still believes in that.

Pause.

The books that I've written,
I burnt,

Background

the grand designs for changing the world ,
the utopian social theory
and how it could become reality.
I burnt them
before others could,
because they couldn't handle ideas any more.

Pause.

You think we shouldn't be too refined for shit
if we want decent fertilizer,
don't you, Helmut.
But I don't believe in us any more, in we,
the great whole and
us being able to change anything.

Laughs.

All I believe in now is contingency.
Mistakes, errors, imponderables,
they make an impression on me.
And as for what you'd call making sense of it all,
I leave that to the politicians,
I leave making sense of it all
To the scientists.
And see the results.
Cloned sheep with rheumatism.
Collapsing towers.
Genocide in the heart of Africa.

Walks over to him and looks over his shoulder.

And occasionally a particularly fine piece of jewellery.

Pause.

Television. Fighting in the street.

Look at these children.
They haven't understood

that politics isn't made on the streets.

They're playing straight into the President's hands

with their demonstrations.

If demonstrations did any good,

then people would be on the streets all the time;

everywhere, day and night, there'd be

demonstrations for or against something.

Look at that,

tear gas everywhere,

water cannon everywhere,

and these kids everywhere.

Look at these kids –

Silence. HELMUT absorbed in his work. ELLA gives him a gentle clip on the back of the head.

I was like that once –

I can recognize myself,

albeit in a distorted form.

With you on the other hand

nothing has changed.

No change for decades,

not even the slightest thing.

But that's what I love about you.

Constancy. Reliability.

The complete absence of questions.

Self-doubt, world weariness, pioneer spirit,

lots of white space on your map.

Gives him a soft clip on the back of the head.

(Romantic.)

Do you remember –

My core.

Silence.

The core of my theory used to be –

The core of my theory is now –

the unreliable world.
The only book I haven't burnt.

Pause.

The only book I could believe in.
On television the President again.

Economics and science,
they're the religions of our times.
They say economy and mean growth,
they say economy and mean profit.
Capital,
another word that's gone out of fashion.
Last Christmas
my bank sent me a letter
With a recipe for Christmas biscuits.
Oh great, capital is thinking of me,
capital wants to make sure
my biscuits turn out alright.
Perhaps I should
invite capital round to our house,
what do you think, Helmut,
so that we can get to know each other,
and we can become friends.

Pause.

How do they appeal to small clients in
let's say, Manila.
How to make shoes out of rubber tyres.
How to repair bank notes.
How to build corrugated iron huts
to withstand a monsoon.

Silence. The PRESIDENT continues to speak soundlessly.

Unreliability.
Resistance.

Pause.

Some of my colleagues now have their own talk show.
At night. At night a couple of viewers want to know
What a philosopher looks like in the flesh.

Pause.

I turn the sound off.
I watch these mouths,
how they can form words without any doubts. Amazing.

Pause.

The humanities gave up resistance
long ago.

Clips HELMUT on the back of the head.

But we're not bothered about that,
are we, Helmut.
We have other worries.
Is this a flawless stone.
The basis of a perfect gem.

Pause.

The sciences can answer everything,
the humanities don't answer anything any more.
The humanities don't even ask questions,
the humanities just fade away.
The humanities are neither effective
nor successful
and that gets to them.
Can there be egg cells without an egg,
can there be life with cloned genes,
can you think without a brain,
the sciences can answer everything,
rather, they don't answer it,
but they find a proof for each different answer.
I'm not going to deny myself the sciences
any longer,
I'm going to join

the sciences

the scientists,

I'm going to fuck a scientist

and get smarter.

Following the insight:

That it's nurture, not nature that makes the difference.

Laughs.

The sciences

which claim to be most important

now call themselves Bio Sciences.

Laughs.

Everything's in there,

and out comes

a new person.

Doesn't it, Helmut.

Clips him on the back of the head.

A new person,

who's supposed to solve all the old problems.

The President's speech.

Silence.

I am watching you, Big Brother.

I am watching you.

5. FOUND

FADOUL at a bus stop, looks through a waste paper basket, then sits down and waits; kicks a plastic bag which is under the bench. Kicks it again deliberately a couple more times, trying to work out what is inside. Bends down, after some hesitation pulls out the bag; there are other bags inside it. FADOUL looks around. He puts the bag back under the bench. But he's too curious or too bored and pulls it out again. Fumbles the openings apart, is just about to look inside when the girl comes and also sits down at the bus stop. FADOUL slides the bag inconspicuously back into its original position. Silence.

GIRL	Have you found an umbrella.
FADOUL	An umbrella.
GIRL	Yes, an umbrella. For the rain, or the sunshine. A para-pluie, a para-sol, an umbrella. Don't you know what an umbrella is.
FADOUL	There's no umbrella here, Madame.

Pause.

GIRL	Have you found a book.
FADOUL	A book.
GIRL	Yes, a book. A thing you read. I left it lying here. Together with the umbrella. Half an hour ago. I got the bus to the harbour and left the umbrella and the book behind. *(Pause.)* The book is called 'The Unreliable World.'
FADOUL	It's not here. No book, no umbrella. Someone's taken them both and disappeared.
GIRL	You're lying. You've found something and you're lying.
FADOUL	But Madame, you can see for yourself, it's just an old bag full of rubbish lying under the bench, it's not mine.
GIRL	No I don't see. I can't see.
FADOUL	You can't see?
GIRL	Are you deaf. *(Pause.)* Stop trying to cheat me. You've hidden the book in the bag.

FADOUL	I don't hide books. And definitely not one which I take it is written in Braille.
GIRL	You've hidden the umbrella in the bag.
FADOUL	Pfff, on a day when there's no sign of rain in any direction. On a day when there's no sunshine in any direction, I would steal an umbrella.
GIRL	There are people who think of tomorrow and plan ahead.
FADOUL	You really are blind, aren't you. *(Laughs.)* You realise, Madame, I'm black, and I'm a foreigner and I work in the docks without a permit and if I go and steal an umbrella or a book or anything else without a permit, then I'd be an idiot who would get deported and if I went and stole an umbrella or a book from a blind person without a permit, then I'd be a stupid black bastard who deserves to be drowned in the harbour. Now I've said everything.

Silence.

I could lend you my jacket. To keep out the rain that's going to fall tomorrow.

Silence.

Please, look in the bag. *(He slides it over to her.)* Go ahead, get your hands dirty, just don't try to clean them on me afterwards.

GIRL	Every day someone tries to cheat me, short-changing me or something, someone I don't know tries to rip me off and if I stand in front of them and force an answer out of them, then they're shocked by their own lack of consideration. At Christmas they're good citizens and give money to the lifeboat men.

Pause.

FADOUL	Why the lifeboat men.

GIRL	People are always getting into danger along the coast here. There's always someone needs help along the coast here.

Pause.

FADOUL	Help. *(Pause.)* They cut a thief's hand off where I come from and if he carries on stealing, then they cut off the other hand too. And if he commits perjury, they'll cut out his tongue, and if he commits adultery, they'll stone him. And if he kills, he is executed. A thief would be long gone, with his legs under his arm, and that shows you don't know people, Madame.
GIRL	Don't be angry. I believe you. *(Pause.)* Is there another punishment in your country.
FADOUL	There are a lot more punishments and there are even punishments which not even the learned know. The judges are highly inventive.
GIRL	And is there also the punishment that people are blinded. And if there is this punishment and people are blinded, what is their crime?

Silence.

GIRL	What kind of crime can someone commit just with their eyes.

Silence.

FADOUL	He can see something that isn't meant to be seen and be unable to remain silent about it.
GIRL	Then it wouldn't have been him who committed the crime, rather those doing what wasn't meant to be seen.
FADOUL	The judges may see it differently. The judges view things with the eyes of justice and justice for us is the sharia. And even if justice only walks on one leg and only has one eye to see with, it never falters and it never falls, never.

GIRL	Here the eyes of justice have been blindfolded, it's a long story, it comes from the Romans.

FADOUL laughs.

GIRL	You're very tactful.

Pause.

FADOUL	Because I don't ask questions.

The girl nods.

FADOUL	I almost asked. I almost asked, who it was who blindfolded your eyes, but now I'm not going to, Madame.
GIRL	Why do you keep calling me Madame.
FADOUL	I don't know, do people not say that. I'm trying to be polite. The way you do, speaking to a stranger who you would like to become less of a stranger.
GIRL	Is my voice so deep that I sound like a Madame.
FADOUL	Your voice is so deep it's perfect. Absolute.
GIRL	*(Laughs.)* Absolute.
FADOUL	That's right. *(Laughs.)*
GIRL	*(Laughs.)* No, you've just guessed my name. I'm called Absolute. The perfect one.
FADOUL	Pleased to meet you, Absolute, absolutely, my name is Fadoul.

They shake hands.

GIRL	If the bus to the docks comes now, I'll just let it go. *(Pause.)* Unless you want to go to the docks too.
FADOUL	Yes, but I – I'm waiting for my friend. My friend is buying newspapers. You know, yesterday there was an accident and today we're looking to see if it's in the newspapers.
GIRL	To see how the blame is apportioned.
FADOUL	To know how knowledge about the blame is apportioned. Whether we need to be afraid of

	sleepless nights; my friend is afraid of sleepless nights provided by his conscience.
GIRL	What sort of accident was it.
FADOUL	People are always getting into danger along the coast here. People always need help along the coast here. *(Laughs.)* Let's see, maybe we'll find a little forgotten drop of something, Absolute, in this old bag, to toast our meeting. *(He pulls out the bag.)*
FADOUL	Just rubbish. *(More and more bags come out.)* Nothing but rubbish in these bags. *(Pulls one bag out of another, pauses, annoyed and goes to the waste paper basket.)* I'll buy us a little bottle at the kiosk. *(Is about to throw everything away, glances at the contents. (Starts, looks more closely, stirs around inside the bag.)* Holy shit –
GIRL	What is it, what's the matter –, what have you found, Fadoul.

FADOUL gathers up the bags and takes them out of the waste paper basket. He sits on the opposite side of the bench, the bags pressed to his body out of the girl's reach.

FADOUL	Rubbish, filth, rubbish, filth.

The bus comes. Absolute stays calmly seated and lets it go on, FADOUL overcomes the impulse to get on and disappear.

GIRL	*(Laughs.)* If you were a thief, that would have been your chance, you'd be gone now with an inconspicuously late departure.
FADOUL	*(Absent-minded.)* Yeah, sure.
GIRL	I believe I trust you. I trust and believe you.

Silence. FADOUL tries to sneak a glance inside the bag.

GIRL	I work at the docks too. Albeit with a permit and I love my permit very much, I must say.
FADOUL	What –
GIRL	I dance. I dance in a bar in the docks. I have a little round stage with a glittering gold pole in the

middle and when the music begins, it belongs just to me, and I dance for men who want to watch me.

Silence.

GIRL   The pole is my helper, it's my orientation, my support, my compass. It's my white stick. And of course it's also everything else and especially what you can now imagine.

Silence.

GIRL   Are you disappointed.

FADOUL   Naked. You are naked when you dance.

GIRL   I take my clothes off, except for a g-string, that covers my privates. And on my breasts I have little gold stars that are just big enough to –

FADOUL   Alright, alright.

GIRL   You're shocked.

FADOUL   Pfff, not in the least, where I come from, we have these things – on every corner, it's practically –

GIRL   A custom.

FADOUL   Yes, it's so common there isn't any expression for it – – . Wow, you're a fully-fledged, hard-boiled stripper anointed with every oil, dear, dear –

GIRL   Do you want to watch me.

FADOUL   Me – Never. That sort of thing blinds you. Blinds you with a red hot poker, till it hisses.

GIRL   *(Takes his hand.)* Look at me please, I want you to look at me, my whole body.

FADOUL   Yes, but not with other men, I'm not a –

GIRL   So you want to look at me when we're alone; when I'm dancing only for you, then you'll look at me.

FADOUL   Yes, that's possible, I might, yes, I think I could be persuaded.

GIRL   Fadoul, I will dance for you alone, I will take all my clothes off for you alone but first you've got to look at me like all the other men. And you've got to see how all the other men look at my whole

	body: when I walk past them in the street, they do it shyly and secretly, because they think I can't tell they're looking; and this secrecy is an insult to me; but when I dance for them in the bar, then they look at me openly and I know that they're looking at me and they desire me and then I respect them.
FADOUL	And I'm supposed to be like the others, I'm supposed to look at you like the others do. I don't understand.
GIRL	But you are like the others. And that's why I might be able to love you. Or do you think you're not like the others. If you think you're not like the others, then I can't love you.
FADOUL	I'm a bit like the others. But I'm also a bit different. No, if I'm honest, I'm definitely different. No, if I'm honest, I am like the others. Ok, I am like the others.
GIRL	If you are like the others, I'll tell you that I dance in the Blue Planet so you can come and see me, every night at midnight. And now tell me where you live, so that I can visit you and fetch you if you don't come to the Blue Planet.
FADOUL	We, we live in a tower block, my friend Elisio and I. In the office block opposite the petrol station, as long as it's empty, before it gets knocked down.
GIRL	The suicide tower.
FADOUL	The asbestos tower.
GIRL	If the bus to the docks comes now, I'm going to get on.
FADOUL	I've got to wait for my friend.
GIRL	I know. *(Pause.)* And you've got to look in the bag.

The bus comes. Absolute gets on. FADOUL looks in the bag. Silence.

ELISIO enters with a newspaper, umbrella and book.

| ELISIO | Look what I've found. It's in Braille. |

6.TO JUMP OR NOT TO JUMP

Sleep For ever Rest for ever

A bit macabre

Yes Definitely yes

But you don't know

Could be

But you don't know

Nobody knows But could be

Pause.

This gonna work Imagine endless sleep or something That's boring No

No one for it

Why not Peace at last What you always wanted

Yeah But not permanently Not for ever Can't imagine it anyway

You might not

What now

Pause.

Eternity's not long Once you're into it eternity you don't notice any more don't even know what time is Stop thinking in days and hours If somebody comes along and asks you what time it is you just look at him and say huh

Yeah sure sure

No need to be frightened of tomorrow for example cos there is no tomorrow no next week next year doesn't exist everything's now everything's in the moment if it's not in the moment it doesn't exist

Yeah sure sure

Silence.

But memory

Hm

There's still memory

Pause.

Of course

There's still yesterday there's still last week last year too

Of course

See it's not all now

The other stuff's just in your head Stuff from before

Doesn't matter where it is if it hurts What's the difference if it's the knee or The inner ear if it hurts

Pause.

I want rid of it all everything that hurts everything from before it's got to go

Silence.

Stop hang on Stop we've gone the wrong way I think it's like this In eternity there's no yesterday If there's no tomorrow there's no yesterday either makes sense It's all one and the same Always now I told you

Sounds weird somehow It's like you're sleeping If that's what it is I mean if it's just one day that never ends or keeps on repeating itself and you never know where the end is and where the beginning I don't think that sounds good

Pause.

If I think how glad I am usually when a day like that is over and then there would only be one and it would never come to an end no it doesn't sound good

That's what I'm trying to explain It's the one moment when you feel good you imagine something pleasant all around you candy floss no bad energies no grief like being on drugs pretty much

Yeah sure sure

Ergo And now this moment never ends that's the trick that's the thing an incredible prolonged fucking orgasm into eternity

That'll kill me

You'll never want to come down You'll never want
to come down

And what about hell and eternal damnation and
bad karma and reincarnation and all that shit

Suppose so

Ask one of them priests one of them mufti one of
them Buddhists

Have any of them been there have any of them
seen it with their own eyes

D'you not know this when you're actually already
dead Everyone's given up on you Mum and Dad
are crying by the bed The doctor shakes his head
darkly and you're hovering over the whole scene
kicked right out of yourself sucked right down the
tunnel to the other side towards the light Now
you're hanging up there over yourself and can see
the doctor's bald patch

I know

And what do you say

They weren't really dead I just say Has this got to
do with science I just say Is this serious That's all
mixed up from the last page

Yeah sure sure

Silence.

And what about your previous life

Suppose so

Can you remember Will you be able to remember
if there is such a thing as memory can you
remember it

Think so

What happened you know and not forget

No in eternity you've got to have some idea who
you are and you're not someone else

Yeah sure sure

Silence.

What do you think
What happens then don't know not sure
Nobody knows
It's a risk
I agree
Nobody knows
What do you think yes or no
More yes the risk's more yes
Nobody knows
Well we're going to find out
Yeah sure sure

7. FRAU HABERSATT'S CASES II

Few people running down the street

towards me

They shout ohoh getoutgetout

Or they shout

nothing

I don't understand don't understand

The child pulls my hand

and

I'd only just gone out with the dog

Something's coming this way

And what

There shots where shots where

How do I know where to go

A w-woman throws herself down on the ground out

of her plastic bag roll o-oranges e-eggs

smash

The harsh crack of the shells

the dog licks at them

Where are you going to run what are you going to do

The man next to me breaks he breaks away there's blood sprayed on the walls

I throw myself and the child under me it was already red

Straight down on the do-dog shit straight down

on the dog shit such pain

in my arm suddenly it doesn't hurt hurt

only later

And seven were dead

I'M SORRY

I'VE NOT INTRODUCED MYSELF

MY NAME IS HABERSATT

No I didn't see the boy

only his legs his boots they

were quite clean but

My face on the pavement the black do-dog shit

the egg yolk the blood from my arm a-all over the place this

black red gold that was weird

AND I'M

What I'll never forget the

noise from the automatic I'll never be able

I said turn over turn over turn over to another channel come on

I'M

And his ey-ey his eye was lying next to me

on the pavement all alone and it was looking at me

staring well it couldn't blink any more

UDO'S MOTHER

Silence.

I don't want to talk to her any more no one can

force me no one can

Seven dead twenty-one injured I wasn't

hurt but

UDO THE GUNMAN

The shock comes later and stays forever

and now they want to give us psychological counselling but I don't want them and their psychological counselling

they can go and

always reminding me always reminding me always always

OH HE WAS CALLED ACHIM RIGHT

Oooh pfff well

course it's difficult for the mother

of the perpetrator

it's always tricky

YES

I'M ACHIM'S MOTHER

I'M ASKING YOUR FORGIVENESS

IF THAT'S ALRIGHT

She accuses herself of all these things

all the mistakes and all that

FORGIVENESS

An ordinary printer's secretary

not much time for her son I suspect and

I think you've really got to look at society as a whole and

I ALWAYS TOLD HIM ACHIM I SAID

THOSE STAINS WON'T COME OUT AT SIXTY DEGREES

And suddenly suddenly don't know I don't know

he'd run out of ammunition or something

puts the gun in his mouth and pulls the trigger

I saw it I saw it I saw it puts

IT WASN'T EVIL OF ME

He could have lived in theory albeit severely h-handicapped

HE ALWAYS SPILT EVERYTHING WITH HIS RIGHT

The w-wound in my arm has almost healed

IT WASN'T EVIL OF ME

And pulls the trigger I saw it I saw it

it just flew backwards like the lid off a pressure cooker

just flies away and everything comes out all over the place

THE SMELL OF DAMP OF FRESHLY

Not a word was true not a word about her
guilt the mother's guilt if only it was that simple
but she had lost her child too
ultimately
MY SON WROTE POETRY
YOU OUGHT TO KNOW THAT
I went round and collected
Not all not all
But ten of the survivors gave a d-donation
and a couple of the relatives
Nothing happened to me in the end you've got
to understand
only the dog is disturbed
Eight hundred euros they collected are they mad
I didn't give anything
Yes it was a nice gesture
We were thinking of a week
in Spain
something like that
IT'S PRACTICALLY NOTHING
WE'VE LOST TOUCH UNFORTUNATELY

Silence.

I PUT THE ENVELOPE ON THE BENCH
UNOPENED WHAT DO YOU TAKE ME FOR

Silence

I KNOW WHAT'S MINE AND WHAT'S NOT
MINE

Pause.

IT'LL ALL GET CLAIMED BY THE STATE
EVENTUALLY
And then this weird thing happened
the gunman's mother got in touch with me

when I lost my little one my Alexander

she came after the funeral

I mean the real mother

and it turns out this other one this Frau Habersatt

she isn't a mother at all

I mean

not anyone's

IT'S PRACTICALLY NOTHING

WE'VE LOST TOUCH UNFORTUNATELY

Well we made a complaint

as if it wasn't enough

she looked up the cases in the newspaper

and goes round claiming to be the criminal's mum

she's done the lot

mad isn't it rapists murderers

and the gunman that was the end

for her

I KNOW WHAT'S MINE AND WHAT'S NOT MINE

And now she needs psychiatric treatment I think

and now she's on probation

out there

IT'LL ALL GET CLAIMED BY THE STATE EVENTUALLY

8. GOD IN A BAG

FADOUL   Not a word to Elisio yet. My hiding place for the
money is behind one of the asbestos sheets and
my mouth is – sewn shut. *(Pause.)* My first thought,
forgery. How do 200.089 euros 77 cents end up
under a bench in a bus stop. Two-hun-dred-thou-
sand euros. In used notes. Plus eighty-nine euros
seventy-seven cents in coins. So I take one of the
50-euro-notes – four thousand 50-euro-notes – and
buy cigarettes in a supermarket where they have
one of those machines. I tell the assistant, look
at me, I'm black as the varnish on a piano and
look at this note, a 50-euro-note, in your position
I would put this note under your lamp as fast as
possible because it's probably not genuine. She
refuses, she says she's not a racist, she looks at me
and says she trusts me. Why. It's not a question of
trust, I tell her, it's a question of experience. Or
not. She says, she doesn't understand why I want
to provoke her she's got nothing against foreigners.
Good, I say, great, I say, now please do your duty
and test whether this note is genuine; there are
rules, aren't there, that every 50-euro-note has to
be tested for its genuineness or is there a special
bonus for black people, do I get preferential
treatment because I'm black or something. She
said, to see if it's genuine, there's no such word as
genuineness, and she would have tested the note
herself ages ago if I hadn't said such stupid things
to her right from the start, because she doesn't let
people say stupid things to her, not even black
people. I, confused by this white dialectic, say
why has she been specially nice to me although I
get on her nerves; if someone gets on my nerves,
I am deliberately not nice to them, and she says
yes, that's exactly what you're trying to achieve,
you want me to lose my temper because I've been
provoked, I say, why would I provoke you, I just

want to know if she knows whether this note is genuine or not and I want to know too so that we can all sleep peacefully again and she says, in a challenging way, then go to a bank and you'll find out and I say I've just come from a bank, I've just been to the bank, but I don't trust them and she looks at me and says, stupid arsehole and puts the note under her lamp and says, it's genuine and I say, thanks love, thought so.

Silence.

I'm a simple person. I don't understand anything about – politics. Or science. But I was brave enough to run away. What I know I've left behind me.

Pause.

And all this, me, what I am, who I am and how I am, my entire life, is dependent on a single letter. My life, my fate are dependent on this single letter: A-m-erican A-f-rican.

There you have my life in two words.

Pause.

I'll tell you what I believe.

Long Pause.

God is in this bag.

Pause.

And there's no proof of God except ourselves.

Why: If we'd saved the woman from the sea then she would have been convinced that it was not God's will to let her die, that it was God's hand that helped her, through us. *(Pause.)* That's the way it is: if something wonderful happens to us, something good and unforseen, that we can't explain, then we believe in a force we call God. If misfortune strikes us, then we think God has died.

But I say it's us. Us. God is in us. His power lies within us. What remains of us isn't our hair, our smell and our beauty, but our deeds, good or bad; what we've done or not done, spoken, thought, that's what you'll remember.

You'll remember this moment, when I look into your eyes and tell you: God is within you.

And God is in me, I know that now. I know it, because God sent me this bag. And himself, in this bag. A dirty bag full of used 50-euro-notes. Two hundred thousand euros. Plus eighty-nine euros seventy-seven cents in coins. *(Pause.)* God cannot want me to take the money to the police. Because the police are not God, the police cannot tell truth from lies, unless they have witnesses and an A-frican is no witness for the truth, not anywhere in the world. So they will take the money away from me and as a reward Lufthansa will take me home. God can't want that and I don't want it either.

I've opened my ears. I listen. The God in the bag says: get on with it! Take this money!

And the God inside me answers: I'll do something big! I'll create something people aren't going to forget!

With this bag!

9. FRANZ SHOWS HIS WORK, FRAU ZUCKER SHOWS A SOFT HEART, ROSA SHOWS HER BODY

At FRANZ and ROSA's. FRAU ZUCKER has now had her left foot amputated. On the television the President is muted, and the image distorted.

FRAU ZUCKER   If I worked in a petrol station –

Silence.

FRAU ZUCKER   If I worked in a petrol station –

ROSA   Oh, Mum.

Silence.

FRAU ZUCKER   If I worked in a petrol station, all it would take is one cigarette to blow everything sky high. *Pause.* That's what I think sometimes. *Pause.* But at home I don't even have gas. Where am I supposed to begin.

ROSA   It's your house too.

FRAU ZUCKER   So?

ROSA   Do you want to blow us up too.

Pause.

FRAU ZUCKER   Why not.

ROSA   Mum!

FRAU ZUCKER   That's one thing you're not. I am a mother, you aren't. And the way I see it, you're never going to become one.

ROSA   But you said – . And how are we supposed to then, with you in one room –

FRAU ZUCKER   It wouldn't have stopped me. Your father and I, we conceived you in the middle of an air raid, in the shelter. Your father had just been demobbed as war wounded, we were packed in tight with the smell of people all around us, they were holding their breath, not because of the bombs, because of the conceptions which were taking place right

	in the middle of them. We did it surrounded by all these strangers and I was already over forty but still we tried everything –
ROSA	Mum, you were a small child at the end of the war.
FRAU ZUCKER	Maybe, maybe. But it could have been like that – No, I think it happened that time at the demo for renationalization. As a communist I was definitely pro-renationalization and had chained myself to the bars on the post office window. Your father had also chained himself to the bars and we were hanging there by our arms like Christ on the cross but our lower bodies were absolutely uninhibitedly mobile and gave way to their desires –
ROSA	I think that must be the seventh different version in the last three days.
FRAU ZUCKER	It might have been like that. It could very well have happened that way. I must have conceived at least one of my four children in an unforgettable way. *(Watches the President.)* Not in some dull night with your eyes closed covered in lukewarm sweat. And the only thing you can remember the morning after is some intrusion which interrupted your sleep.

Silence.

ROSA	He doesn't even know my face. And I no longer know his hand on my face. And I don't know anything at all about his hand, how it might be if it touched anywhere on my body.

FRAU ZUCKER watches the President.

FRAU ZUCKER:	I think you can tell with people whether they were conceived in a lukewarm night in a lukewarm bed by mistake or whether they have a passionate justification for being on the planet.
ROSA	He doesn't recognize me.
FRAU ZUCKER	Look at me. *(Pause.)* Rosa, you're not a fighter. You didn't get that from me. Even on one leg I'm still a whole woman. You on the other hand are

completely unerotic on two legs. Here, I'll give you my lipstick.

ROSA weeps.

FRAU ZUCKER   Dear, dear, dear. *(Pause.)* I know I make things difficult for you. I'm sorry. Should I pretend to be dead.

ROSA   *(Gains control of herself.)* Franz should fix that television.

FRAU ZUCKER   The opposite more like. He should smash it to bits. *(Pause.)* I don't need entertainment, not me, I can do all that myself.

ROSA weeps again.

FRAU ZUCKER   To want is to have, Rosa. You need to tell yourself that every night.

ROSA   I want life to carry on. I want that so much.

FRAU ZUCKER   Maybe we can put the cot under the sink if we move the rubbish bin over to one side. What's got to go has got to go, that's what I keep saying to my leg.

FRANZ enters, carrying an urn which he places on a shelf with many other urns.

FRAU ZUCKER   A lot of unclaimed corpses around, eh.

FRANZ   Some of them don't get collected. Some of them nobody wants. As if nobody had ever known them. But I knew them, I took their clothes off and washed them; I combed their hair, arranged their dentures and put their last shirts on. I know them like no-one else ever knew them.

ROSA   Franz, you can't bring all the forgotten urns home.

FRANZ   Yes I can.

ROSA   But what are we supposed to do with them.

FRANZ   Remember.

ROSA   And you think no-one remembers anything at the cemetery.

FRANZ	No, no-one stands in front of a plaque with no name on it.
FRAU ZUCKER	*(Bangs on the television.)* A petrol pump and a cigarette, one decent explosion and that's it.
FRANZ	There are more and more dead people. More and more dead people who haven't been collected.
FRAU ZUCKER	*(To ROSA.)* Think of the bars on the windows. *(She puts a cloth over her face.)*
FRANZ	*(Watches the President.)* Two more suicides today. Two suicides. Jumped off the same tower block.
ROSA	*(Turns off the President.)* Franz, think about something else.
FRANZ	Life, just one long wait for death. And I, I've made waiting my profession. *(Pause.)* A beautiful profession.
ROSA	*(Unbuttons her dress.)* A cook in the kitchen and a whore in the bedroom.

The two suicides enter, naked. While FRANZ is speaking, they lie down on the table and he washes them with great care, their faces, each limb individually.

FRANZ	The better off we are, the more dead. The more things improve, the more people volunteer for death. That's strange. *(Pause.)* When things are going badly we're all quiet.
ROSA	*(Pulls her dress over her shoulders, pauses.)* If you don't look at me, I'm not going to move.
FRANZ	And I, I apply myself, I waste myself on behalf of the dead. All for the dead.

ROSA drops her dress, takes off all her clothes and lies down between the two corpses.

ROSA	I thought you might look at me.
FRANZ	At first I thought I had to be quick. Create a new life for every dead person.
ROSA	Not that you would turn towards me, no, that's too much to expect. But you might look at me.

FRANZ	But I place my hands on their skin and abstinence bites through my hands deep into my body.
ROSA	And you might say your hair is such a nice colour today –

FRANZ has finished the washing without having touched ROSA. He combs the two bodies to the left and right of her.

FRANZ	With the sick I lacked the compassion. Compassion just didn't happen. And that's why I couldn't hurt their bodies. I couldn't injure them. I couldn't heal them. *(Pause.)* Now they don't need compassion any more. I've washed the last remnants of life out of them. And in the end I seal their bodily openings and let them go. *(Pause.)* Do you understand that, Rosa.

He has finished combing. Seals the bodily openings. He too lies down next to the two dead people to sleep. Silence.

ROSA	Or, you've made a really good job of ironing your blouse, all so accurate and loving. Or that he might put a flower in the vase for me along with the artificial one. Just one. And I wouldn't even want to know whether it had come from the last rites. And if he wanted to touch me, we could find a place in the cemetery where we were alone and everything could stay hidden, and no-one would need to know a thing…and then one day perhaps there could be a single little chocolate by my plate at breakfast, a Ferrero Rocher or a Mon Cherie, and I would sit looking at it knowingly for a while, before putting it in my jacket pocket and keep putting my fist round it till I can feel it melting, my Mon Cherie…

Silence.

If I had money, if I really had a lot of money, then once a month I would stay in a hotel, in one of those hotels where you walk into the room and the television has writing on it saying *Welcome, Rosa*, where the bedcovers have been pulled back and there's a sweet on your pillow …

10. *ABSOLUTE*

FADOUL and ELISIO's place. Only ELISIO is present, he is sleeping. ABSOLUTE enters, quietly, carefully.

ABSOLUTE   Fadoul – Fadoul –

She finds the sleeping ELISIO and feels his face, thinks she recognizes FADOUL, feels his body above and underneath the cover, over and under his clothes; ELISIO reacts in his sleep, instinctively, delighted, tenderly, until...

ABSOLUTE   My book. You've got my book. Stolen. Fadoul, you cheated me, stole from me – *(She comes out from under the covers with the book in her hand.)*

ELISIO   *(Opens his eyes.)* What a dream –

ABSOLUTE   *(Listens.)* Say that again –

ELISIO   What a dream –

ABSOLUTE   Oh oh oh – *(Pause.)* I think I've confused you with someone else. Oh oh oh, that is embarrassing. Why didn't you say anything.

ELISIO   I was dreaming.

ABSOLUTE   Where did you get this book.

ELISIO   I found it. At a newspaper kiosk. Together with an umbrella.

Pause.

ABSOLUTE   Where's Fadoul.

ELISIO   Am I his keeper.

ABSOLUTE   He didn't come to the Blue Planet. I was waiting.

ELISIO   So. He'll have had his reasons.

ABSOLUTE   What sort of reasons.

Silence.

ABSOLUTE   I've got a cross on my calendar. Three days ago, when I met him at the bus stop. I've waited three nights. Another night and I'll be too old.

Silence.

ABSOLUTE	Am I annoying you.
ELISIO	I don't know anything about you and I don't know anything about him any more, not since you met at the bus stop. He comes to work during the day and at night he either sleeps on his feet or paces up and down. And if I say a word to him, he looks at me like this, sideways... So, yes, you are annoying me. You've woken me up and I tried so long to get to sleep.

Silence.

ELISIO	If you come here then I'm going to have to look after you and that annoys me more than trying to get to sleep.
ABSOLUTE	Then tell Fadoul I was here and if he wants me he should come to the Blue Planet. If he doesn't want me – tell him – don't say anything. *(Silence.)* No, you better not say anything. *(Silence.)*
ELISIO	I was only dreaming.
ABSOLUTE	What am I saying. I've never talked like this. Three days ago I danced, the day before yesterday I danced, yesterday I danced, every night I waited and hoped that Fadoul would come and watch me. I've never hoped for three nights in a row before. Mostly I only have to hope for one night, two at the most, but three, never.
ELISIO	Don't come here again. Without eyes, this is a death trap. With eyes it's dangerous, but without eyes it's deadly. *(Pause.)* Last week four people died here. Four of them. One of them was beaten to death, another shot himself to heaven through a vein. And two jumped off the roof. *(Silence.)* They die like flies that only live for a day. Like flies. Like flies. Like flies. What's the difference.
ABSOLUTE	Flies do at least see things from three thousand angles, and that's with each eye, before they put them together to make a complete image. Six

	thousand different views of everything that exists create their image of the world.
ELISIO	Do they die any cleverer than us. Or do they just get a nicer view.
ABSOLUTE	Well they see more than I do.

They laugh. Pause.

ELISIO	What would you do, being blind, if someone else were to have an accident right in front of your blind eyes. And your help, being blind, came too late. What would you do.
ABSOLUTE	I'd wish I was a fly.
ELISIO	To escape.
ABSOLUTE	So someone would swat me. *(Pause. ABSOLUTE laughs hard, desperately.)* That's what you want to hear. I don't know what happened. All I know is you've managed to find unhappiness. And now you want everyone to confirm it for you.
ELISIO	You're even crueller than you look. *(Pause.)* A woman drowned and it was my fault. Quite simple.
ABSOLUTE	You're wrong. *(Laughs.)* It wasn't your fault. The most you've got is a guilty conscience.
ELISIO	Isn't that enough. It's enough for me not to get any sleep.

ABSOLUTE opens the book, finds a marked page. A crumpled newspaper cutting falls out of the book, ELISIO picks it up.

ABSOLUTE	*(Reads.)* 'We attempt to find an explanation for events around us, for our lives, for the happenings of the world ex post facto, in the hope that if we can apply these universal rules, we might influence the future. But these causal links are only ever apparent in retrospect and no one, neither us, nor God, nor even nature itself possesses any knowledge abut how we will develop together. We might as well throw dice.' *(Pause.)* This book is called *The Unreliable World.*

While this is happening FADOUL enters.

ABSOLUTE I don't know, I don't know if I can trust this book like a person, whether it is accurate like a picture or whether it is unreliable like a machine or like nature.

ELISIO *(Gives her the article.)* There were strange things in the papers. It said in the paper she had killed herself. Deliberately.

FADOUL Have you noticed it's only ever women do it in water. A man never does it in water. A man looks for a roof or a rope. A man uses a gun if he can find one.

ELISIO Did you ever hear of anybody taking their clothes off and laying their clothes carefully on the bank before going and drowning themselves.

Silence.

ABSOLUTE Maybe she wanted to make it look like an accident. Maybe she was so ashamed, that she didn't want to provoke anyone any more. Maybe she was torn.

FADOUL What does that mean, torn by shame.

ELISIO Torn by shame means when you want a woman but she doesn't want you.

ABSOLUTE Or vice versa.

ELISIO You don't understand and get violent and what gets broken is what was your self-respect and instead of dignity you now have a wound. And it can't be seen on your body. Don't ask such stupid questions. *(Pause.)* We were there, no-one forced the woman to go into the water. But maybe there's a force inside, yeah. *(Pause.)* I've thought about it for a long time and lost sleep but the longer I'm here on this side of the earth, the more I don't understand. How many people kill themselves. Why. Why does someone go looking for death out of weakness. Because they're indoctrinated from an early age, it is not in your hands, the world

	cannot be relied on. Like this book. This book is such crap, Absolute.
FADOUL	Right. I know because I met God.

Both the others stare at him.

| FADOUL | Yes. God is in a bag. I didn't want to say at first, because – it made me uncertain. He wants me to do something great, possibly I should become like him and – well, maybe I need your help. |

Both the others stare at him.

| FADOUL | I've got him hidden at the moment. But I can fetch him any time when you're ready. |

Both the others stare at him.

| FADOUL | Fine, just forget it again. It's not so important. It'll be alright. |

ELISIO goes to ABSOLUTE, takes her finger, taps it against his forehead.

| ELISIO | What did I tell you, completely twisted. *(Pause.)* Absolute, will you give me your umbrella. |
| ABSOLUTE | The one you found and never gave back to me? I'll give it to you. May it rain heavily and often. |

ELISIO takes the umbrella out from under the bed and leaves.

Silence.

ABSOLUTE	Do I know you again. What happened, Fadoul. *(Pause.)* I waited for you, three nights in a row, and you – you talk about God.
FADOUL	Yes. *(Pause.)* About money. Money. Not God. Money.
ABSOLUTE	You just said God was in a bag.
FADOUL	No, money, money's in a bag. Absolute, you're getting everything mixed up. *(Pause.)* I couldn't come and look at you because I found God in a bag and I was completely confused.
ABSOLUTE	So it was God.

FADOUL	Yes, God, of course it was God, what else could it be.
ABSOLUTE	You just said, money was in a bag.
FADOUL	No, God, God is in a bag, do you understand, that's why everything is so complicated.
ABSOLUTE	Show me the bag.
FADOUL	What bag.
ABSOLUTE	The bag with God in it.
FADOUL	There isn't one.
ABSOLUTE	You just said, God is in a bag.
FADOUL	Ye-eees – I did –
ABSOLUTE	So show me the bag.
FADOUL	What bag.
ABSOLUTE	The bag with God in it.
FADOUL	I've hidden it.
ABSOLUTE	Where.
FADOUL	Not telling.

Pause.

ABSOLUTE	Then show me the money.
FADOUL	What money.
ABSOLUTE	The money in the bag.
FADOUL	What bag. *(Pause.)* You're trying to trick me.
ABSOLUTE	How.
FADOUL	With these bags and the money and all this stuff.
ABSOLUTE	Fadoul, does this bag with the money exist.
FADOUL	If God wishes... Allah is great, you know.
ABSOLUTE	Allah is great.
FADOUL	Yes. I have direct experience of that. That's all I can say about it.

Silence.

ABSOLUTE	And that's why you didn't come to the Blue Planet.
FADOUL	Yes.

ABSOLUTE	It wasn't because of me that you didn't come to the Blue Planet.
FADOUL	No.
ABSOLUTE	And if I wait one more night, then tonight I can hope that you will come to the Blue Planet.
FADOUL	Yes, you can.
ABSOLUTE	Waiting all night and then losing hope, that's what makes you old.

Pause.

FADOUL	We behave as if we could understand each other, yes. We'll try. That's the agreement, the agreement that we don't attack each other like animals to satisfy our hunger and our longing for love.
ABSOLUTE	It would be nice to be that sort of animal. Love doesn't know people. Even me, I'm only a person some of the time, love doesn't know me.
FADOUL	Should we try lust.
ABSOLUTE	Lust I can provide myself. My fingers are quick and strong. My fingers know me best.
FADOUL	Then I don't know what we could try.
ABSOLUTE	You said yourself. Hunger. Longing. Loving like animals.

Silence. FADOUL is too incredulous to kiss ABSOLUTE.

FADOUL	Absolute.
ABSOLUTE	What is it.
FADOUL	Absolutely nothing. I'm just saying your name. To get used to it. For the first time in my life I want to get used to something. *(Silence.)* And it's completeness itself.
ABSOLUTE	Fadoul.
FADOUL	What is it.
ABSOLUTE	Nothing. I'm just saying your name.
FADOUL	*(Pleased.)* What the hell, your parents and this name of yours – what kind of people are they, alcoholics.

Silence.

ABSOLUTE   My parents are both blind. They wanted to create me in their image and after they had conceived me, they had my genes analysed to make sure that I would be born blind like them; they wanted us to be the same, they, my parents, and me, their child; because they think they live in a complete world and therefore I should belong to their world and also be complete.

FADOUL   And what do you think.

ABSOLUTE   I think they're right, their world is complete and I am the complete child they wished for. I've made them happy.

FADOUL   Don't you ever want to see.

ABSOLUTE   I want that more than anything else in the world.

Silence.

FADOUL   I will see for you.

ABSOLUTE   Your blue will be different from mine, your sky will be different from mine. I don't know what desert and stone and cities are outside of my eyes, which are night and black when I dream and night and bright when I want them to be.

FADOUL   I'll give you my skin which is black and my hair which is black, my hands, which are black, my thoughts, which are black, my semen, which is black, and my eyes, which are black, and then we're equal, but still different, and we can call that difference love.

ABSOLUTE   Agreed.

11. JUMPED

I didn't know him before. Saw him at a party, the first time. The night it happened. Not my type at first sight. Pushy is exaggerating, but too open, somehow too open. *(Pause.)* He asked me whether I believed in God, we hadn't drunk much, I said, someone would have to prove to me he existed, he gave me this look, whether my life had any meaning. *(Silence.)* He must have been in his early twenties, I thought, he'd just started studying Polish and business studies. Pretty and blond and. A kind of best friend type. *(Silence.)* I did try to answer, honestly, I was a bit drunk, and hyper, then we smoked dope and I told him about my year studying in the Philippines, where I had to amputate a man's gangrenous toes, a beggar, who'd managed to get himself to the aid station, he was lucky, waiting room was full every day, women with botched abortions who had blood running down their thighs, children with stab wounds in their stomachs, old people whose teeth were rotten, glassy-eyed prostitutes who'd been beaten black and blue, babies whose faces had been bitten by rats, blind men whose clothes stank of piss, mothers with dead children that wouldn't come out of their wombs, drunk, their bodies stinking, you could cut them open without an anaesthetic, they'd not notice. Yeah, anyway, I told him about that and that I enjoyed the job and that now I work in a German hospital. Of course it's a lot more routine. *(Pause.)*

Whether life has any meaning for me. He wouldn't let up. I was completely drunk. I didn't spend a lot of time thinking. I said no, it doesn't, life doesn't have any meaning for me, my life doesn't and neither does anyone else's. He said why bother then. I said ok at some point I discovered a talent, an interest, I like cutting people open and seeing what they're like inside, I enjoy putting them back together, I like watching this pretty fucking perfect organism, how it works pretty fucking perfectly, most of the time, and where it doesn't, I imitate its fucking perfection and try to make up for it. Try to make up for. Not because it makes sense but because I'm good at it.

I still think he's definitely the sort of person who doesn't give up quickly; he searches and finds and what he finds he'll hold onto and give it a meaning. That kind of person. I even envied him. I really did envy him.

We didn't talk much more after that. We went back to mine. I need a shower and come back into the kitchen because I've forgotten to give him a drink, so I come in, naked, and he dashes past me, doesn't say anything, doesn't look at me, dashes past me, into the next room, I follow him, it all happens so quick, I don't really realise, all I can see is the open window, the open window – no, I couldn't look down, I couldn't, I must have mentioned it in passing at some point, the sunshine, the light, the view, that I live on the thirteenth floor –

12. ELLA II

HELMUT, ELLA's husband, has a goldsmith's magnifier in his eye and is busy making something very small with his hands. The television shows a speech by the President. ELLA watches with the sound off.

ELLA I have written the President
how many articles, essays even,
letters to his newspaper
and his TV channel.
Answers to his speeches.
And not sent a single one.
Not a single line.
My theory, the theory of underlying particles
says that the structure of social systems,
how they change and develop,
and what that means for the individual
can only be understood
by separating and mapping
micro-sections.
The underlying picture
is what's near at hand.
The revolution comes from the petri dish
and not the other way round.
What is recognizable
is the next small unit.
From there I go further, very
slowly I add on the smallest elements
and weave a net out of them that encompasses everything.
A net of Sisyphus.
The net is never completed,
new unforseen holes are always appearing
the knots providing a structure and form are always changing,

something that was once recognizable and definite can

have completely dissolved tomorrow,

a tear flaps in its place,

but that's also what's wonderful about it.

Pause.

I don't want any supervision

I don't want any philosophical overview

I don't want a seamless explanation of everything,

I hate systems,

I'm going to dedicate myself to fragments

to the flawed, the incomplete, the breaks, the remainders,

what's not understood, what's underlying, what's corrupted

to the smallest most insignificant things.

That's the challenge.

That's life.

That's the challenge of life.

The unreliable world.

Silence. HELMUT is working.

I'm afraid that's misleading.

Maybe even contradictory.

And there's the continual threat

that suddenly a system

is going to appear from somewhere.

Yes, I contradict myself.

Silence.

That's what's so wonderful about it.

Silence.

Whatever happens I'm not going to turn out like you.

Is about to give him a clip on the back of the head but then pauses.

You jeweller.

Silence.

Window chair wall hand
is all that I can say.
Life death meaning
are things I can't say any more.
I can't take those words out of my mouth.
But what does 'meaning' mean.
What does 'chair' mean.

Pause.

The President has a clear advantage.
He says chair
and there's a strike.
He says window
and a trade unionist kills himself.
He says wall
and 150,000 workers avoid redundancy
Something always happens
immediately after the President opens his mouth
a direct reaction follows.
Even though we don't understand him.
The President says something,
and no-one understands him;
the President says something
and nobody knows
what he intends with these words
Or what his words
intend with him.
But something happens.
Immediately.
A phenomenon.
The President
doesn't understand himself
what he says.

A phenomenon.
The President doesn't understand himself
how are we supposed to understand him.
I pity him
but I envy him too.
The self-elected incoherence
in this country.
An illiterate as President,
a footballer, actor, pop star,
it could go on like that for ever.
Polemicizing against it is cheap,
laughing about it is dangerous.
Stupid people think they're stupid,
intelligent people think they're stupid,
and between them madness grows.

Pause.

The country's being ruined,
oh dear.
The world's going to the dogs,
oh dear,
but I'm still,
oh dear,
now I really am quite
optimistic again.
I say that to myself every day.
Maybe it'll help some time.
Eh, Helmut.
Maybe the breakthrough will come some time,
if we carry on flailing around like this.

Gives him a clip on the back of the head.

My husband's a goldsmith.
Goldsmith.

A nice word.

A nice job.

Making jewellery.

An entirely meaningless occupation,

and maybe the only thing that matters:

making the world more beautiful.

Pause.

The seer's advice.

We don't have to understand the world,

we don't take it apart,

we don't even have to change its form,

we simply add something to it,

a little compliment,

a healing flourish,

that makes everything more pleasant.

That's the seer's advice.

Make things pleasant for yourselves.

Have a MORE BEAUTIFUL life.

Silence.

To be honest, I despise my husband.

I don't know what he thinks.

If he thinks at all,

or whether his hands are anticipating his instincts,

if they shape their material,

work it, soften it,

to make it presentable,

and that looking at it you can think,

oh,

so beautiful, haven't seen anything like that for ages.

Then everyone can wonder

Why I married my husband

Even though I don't talk to him,

don't talk,

don't have conversations,

can't.

Gives him a clip on the back of the head.

Because his hands anticipate his instincts,

along me and up and down and keep going,

because they sought me out,

my flesh,

because they worked me like that, softened me like that,

so that I became more presentable,

so people thought when they looked at me,

oh,

in love,

or even,

oh,

loved,

loved loved loved,

or even

oh,

loving and loved, loving and loved,

oh oh oh.

Pause.

One time.

That was a long time ago.

Gives him a clip on the back of the head.

And won't come back again.

Gives him a clip on the back of the head.

A feeling that's been lost once

Can never ever under any circumstances

Be recovered,

not anywhere
not ever.

Silence.

I can say chair
I can say hand
Shoe foot
Cup
Book
Umbrella

Silence.

13. FRAU HABERSATT TRIES TO AVOID PROBATION

Sea fills the horizon. ELISIO goes walking up and down with ABSOLUTE's umbrella and a bunch of flowers, he turns the umbrella upside down and places it on the water, puts the flowers inside and allows them to be carried away. FRAU HABERSATT watches him.

FRAU HABERSATT   The judge says to me: now you've got to go on probation. I asked him what does that mean. He said, leave other people alone and leave other people's pain alone. Find yourself a nice hobby. Live your own life. *(Pause.)* What is my own life. Aren't other people part of that. He couldn't answer that. *(Silence.)*

It could be so easy. I see him near the harbour promenade. He's standing roughly this far away from me. Two arms' lengths. *(Pause.)* I could say something like, *You're not from round here – (Pause.)* No with a stupid sentence like that I would have ruined everything; alright and he says, *You're right, I'm from the South* – and I say, *I like the South, it sounds like – ...*

We would look at each other. And then, as if quite by chance, I say, *You must have left a big family behind there – ...*

He glances out to sea and says, *No, I haven't got any family, my whole family is dead– ...*

I look at the sea and I say –

I could tell him everything, someone who'd until recently been a stranger. That's what I dream of.

Pause.

Life could be that simple, that simple.

Pause.

I'm not going on probation.

Silence.

FRAU HABERSATT   You're not from round here.

ELISIO looks angry and doesn't answer.

FRAU HABERSATT   Where do you come from then.

ELISIO looks away, then makes a vague hand movement in the direction of the horizon. Silence.

FRAU HABERSATT   Aha. *(Pause.)* Something quite different.

Silence.

FRAU HABERSATT   The furthest I've been – *(Points.)* – was Helgoland. *(Pause.)* There's just one house. Cliffs all around it. Very small cliffs. Water all around that. *(Pause.)* There's nothing to do there.

Silence.

FRAU HABERSATT   Walk round the house. Along the cliffs.

ELISIO   Helgoland. Legoland. Toy world. *(Still angry.)* Do a lot of people kill themselves in Helgolegoland.

FRAU HABERSATT   No. Don't think so. *(Pause.)* They jump here, off the suicide tower. Or turn the gas on. Or drown. *(Pause.)* Sometimes there's just no other way.

ELISIO   Yes there is.

FRAU HABERSATT laughs out loud.

ELISIO   There is.

FRAU HABERSATT laughs out loud.

ELISIO   There's always another way.

FRAU HABERSATT   *(Laughs.)* You're a happy person. A happy person from the South.

ELISIO   What do you know. What do you know. What do you know about the South. Living in Legoland. With your building block dreams of houses in Helgoland and the sea. What do you know. What do you know about death –

FRAU HABERSATT laughs nervously.

Silence.

ELISIO   Why are you laughing. Why are you laughing. Why are you laughing at me. I ran away from the South, from the South, yeah, we all come from the South where it's hot and people die like flies without having to kill themselves. In the South they laugh at you. In the South, we laugh at you, we laugh at you and I, I don't understand any of this here –

FRAU HABERSATT cannot move. She remains silent, helplessly.

FRAU HABERSATT   There's not a lot I don't know about death.

Silence. She's shaking.

FRAU HABERSATT   For a long time I've been a grave, an empty grave on legs. Once I was pregnant, with a baby boy. I already had a name for him. He was supposed – He was supposed … *(Moves her mouth.)* …to be called. *(Pause.)* But he died, he died inside my body. Just before birth. I had to bring him into the world dead, my body was a coffin. It's a long time ago.

Silence.

ELISIO   Ten days ago a woman went into the water and drowned, over there – *(Points.)* I saw her, I wanted to save her, but my friend was afraid. We were both afraid. Cowardice kept us dry. *(Pause.)* I've got a picture of her from the newspaper and she comes out of the water every night. I have warm feet, her body and her hair are blue.

Silence.

FRAU HABERSATT   I tell myself maybe it's for the best. He might have done terrible things, maybe he'd have become a thief or even a murderer – and, and I would have been the mother of a criminal my whole life long. My whole life long I'd have to go round apologizing for him. *(Pause.)* And still, still they'd hate me. Wouldn't they. The world would hate me.

ELISIO　　　　　Fadoul, my friend, has fallen in love, with a girl with deep black eyes. Her eyes are black because her black-eyed parents thought they were God.

Silence.

FRAU HABERSATT　　We'd all like to be innocent.

ELISIO　　　　　And then Fadoul found two hundred thousand euros in a bag and he's going to get an operation for the black-eyed girl's eyes; it's going to happen tomorrow in hospital and now he too thinks he's almighty. Suddenly there are so many more Gods around me. Even my friend is a God. I'm the only one who's completely ordinary. And I can't do anything about it. *(Starts crying.)*

FRAU HABERSATT　　*(Approaches him determinedly.)* I'm sorry. I haven't introduced myself. My name is Habersatt. *(Pause.)* Klara Habersatt. *(Silence.)* And no-one has ever called me mother. And also no-one has known my name and abbreviated it affectionately. *(Pause.)* And that's all I know about death.

ELISIO　　　　　Umm –

　　　　　Umm –

　　　　　Ummahat –

The sea washes the umbrella and the flowers ashore.

14. AND EVERYONE

Been here almost an hour. I've been here an hour and a half. Now they've called in the police psychologists and sealed off the area. Would go and choose the motorway bridge wouldn't he. It would have to be the motorway bridge and it would have to be the rush hour. Middle of the rush hour. Can you believe it, can you believe it. It's a woman. It's a man. I'm running late, I'm way too late, I might as well turn round and drive straight home, the boss thinks I've lost it. One twisted woman, one really twisted woman, how does she even get up there. It's a man. Won't let the psychologist character closer than five or six metres. Don't blame her. It's a him. Look around, wow, there must be, at least, kilometres of them, coming from three directions, if each car's only got one person in it that'll make nine, ten thousand people whose day's been ruined by this sick lunatic. I'm not coming again. Forget it. Forget the lot of it. And I thought, today I'll go the back way, honestly, I did, then I saw the sign in front of me, and well, I was late, and now this bollocks. If only she would jump. It's a he. Jump. He doesn't want to. Bet he doesn't want to. Ok, I'll bet you a tenner. If you're gonna jump, then jump. No-one's gonna miss you. Antisocial arsehole. Can't she go into the woods and find a lone tree with a strong branch that'll do the job for her. No, wants to be seen. She wants to be picked off the bridge there by the velvet gloves of the police shrink. She probably wants something completely different. She's probably so dried out and rotten that she needs really hard stuff to feel a little stroking stroking. It's a he, can you get your head round that, it's a he. Got to make a spectacle of his death wish. Suicide exhibitionist. It's a turn on for him. Shoot him. Blow him away off that fucking bridge. He wants to be flown out by helicopter. Blackmailing us with his death, the cunt. Chucking himself under a train would be more socially acceptable, there's an hour's delay while they clear the bits of him off the line and then everyone can carry on. This one here really takes the biscuit. He just doesn't want to die. I can tell by looking at him. He just doesn't want to die. If he waits any longer, I'm going to go up there and bash his skull in myself. Then he'll have got what he wanted. This can go on for hours. Hours.

Come on then, jump, get on with it, everybody on the count of three, one Jump, jump, jump –

15. LIGHT

ABSOLUTE's dressing room at the Blue Planet. Absolute in front of a mirror, on the other side of the mirror ELISIO.

ABSOLUTE   So Fadoul says, I'll give you the money for the operation. The money in the bag. God's bag. He's sent the money to let you see. I say maybe God didn't intend to send the bag, rather he lost it unintentionally and he'd like it back. He's looking for it. Maybe the bag was intended for someone else entirely, how can you tell. Maybe someone else will be very unhappy without this bag. Fadoul says, if that's the case, God would have let us know. This is a sign, a sign from a divine bus stop.

ELISIO   I wanted the images to stop. I wanted forms, shapes, animals, people and colours to stop. I wanted mirrors to stop. Streams, lakes, the sea, ice, glaciers, puddles to stop. Because I was in a cell in my continent's never-ending night, in the darkness of a prison cell, blackness as impenetrable as blackness. *(Pause.)* When it gets light outside, you will have to lift your head, stretch it upwards, where a thin sheet of tin, so high you can't reach it, lets in little white points of sunlight. *(Pause.)* Arrows of light in your eyes, which strengthen the pain of darkness.

ABSOLUTE   I thought about it a long time. I don't believe God exists, don't believe in signs, in fate. I believe in science. And the power of people's desires. There isn't anything else. People took my eyes away and people can give me them back. That's what I believe in.

ELISIO   Gradually I could feel the walls that were holding this blackness together. The ground calmed me when I stretched out on top of it and shut my eyes, wanting to rob the night of a few seconds, powerlessly. And the wall gave me a back when I crouched against it in a gentle, only a very gentle movement that maybe imitated the beating wings of a bird in flight. Heat seeped into the blackness with a soft buzzing. *(Pause.)* And I started scratching away at one of the clay bricks.

ABSOLUTE   And the sky, the starlit sky above me, which I've never seen, has nothing to do with it. *(Pause.)* So I have taken the money, thank you Fadoul, I have no scruples. And then I invited Elisio and Fadoul to the Blue Planet, to dance for them.

One last time.

ELISIO   I tried to dig more holes, with my hands, with one hand, with my fingers, with one finger, with my nails, with the nail on one finger, with a single nail a nail a nail on the clay wall covered in damp scratching clawing scratching with one fingernail, till I reached the light, till I had dug scratched clawed a beam of sunlight out of the wall and it grows into a glowing finger, the finger of light grows out of my prison wall and it shines when I close my eyes, its image vibrates behind my eyelids –

Long Silence.

I want the images to stop. Forms, shapes, animals, people and colours to stop. I want mirrors to stop. *(ad inf.)*

16. RECOGNITION

At FRANZ and ROSA's. FRAU ZUCKER has now had her left leg amputated at the knee. She is in a wheelchair having her afternoon nap. FRAU HABERSATT and ELISIO; the latter has the umbrella with him which he will forget in a corner.

They have already been to four undertakers and explained their case but without any success. Now they are trying a fifth and last time and that's why Elisio and Frau Habersatt are in this tiny room one late afternoon, and Elisio awkwardly takes the now somewhat dilapidated photo of the drowned woman out of the inside pocket of his only smart jacket where he keeps it between two sheets of cardboard specially cut to size for the purpose and says: *Do you know this woman?* Franz studies the photo with keen interest, shakes his head, hands it back to Elisio, then with a movement of his hand demands to see it again, holds it close to his face, then at arm's length and eventually nods. He points carefully with a spotlessly clean index finger at the photo without touching it and says: *On the day I started at Berger's, she was lying in the refrigeration room. She came from the path lab, had been found in the water. She drowned near the docks, where the bank is flat and covered with stones.* Elisio is then silent for a moment and says: *I saw her, I saw her going into the water.* The two men look at each other. Frau Habersatt now has to explain why she has come too, but her mouth is too dry. Elisio says: *This woman wants me to adopt her as my mother, but that's another story.* Frau Habersatt doesn't wish to be the source of any embarrassment: *He thinks, if he can find out who this woman was and why she died, if she died of her own free will, then he might be able to sleep again at night, even though his guilt would remain.* He didn't save her. Franz understands, he'd like to help, he knows the stories of all his dead bodies, he would also reveal this woman's story in order to make someone else's life easier, but: *I remember* this woman because of her red hair but I didn't take care of her. I just saw her lying there, naked, on the slab, ready for the last rites and to be made beautiful, although she didn't need that, because although she'd come out of the water and her flesh was heavy, she was still a beautiful woman, with soft, blue skin and her eyes closed and her breasts and feet leaning outwards. Nobody came forward, no relatives, no friends. And I, I didn't touch her once. Now that I know something about her, that there are two people looking for her, I'm sorry. They cannot see the sadness in Elisio's face because Elisio is too bound up in this case, he says: *Do you know her name at least.* And again Franz has to shake his head. Frau Habersatt can now longer bear the weight of these facts and collapses down on the bed, a brief sigh flies from her throat. Franz says: *She's anonymous and was buried in a poor grave paid for by the city. Now you know everything I know.* Elisio looks at the photo in silence and thinks of the encroaching darkness and the night to come and that the questions have not got any smaller since yesterday. Frau Zucker wakes from her late afternoon snooze and has a shock: *How long have we had visitors. Have I been dribbling. I can't help it, it's diabetes.* Frau Habersatt goes to her and takes her hand to calm her, Frau Zucker is confused: *Am I seeing things, who are these people. I haven't had a stroke, have I, I can't remember them.* Franz says: *My boss sent them, they wanted information about someone who died.* Frau Zucker: *Oh, my son in law brings them all home,* she points to the urns, *please, help yourselves.* And so that the guests do not get the wrong impression, she adds: *I was a Communist, you know, but now I've got diabetes and only one leg and this fellow refuses to get my daughter pregnant, you don't happen to have a place free where you live do you.* Frau Habersatt decides to take a radical step: *I have no children at all, unfortunately, and he doesn't want me either, shall I take you out for a walk.* She pushes Frau Zucker's wheelchair out into the fresh air. Frau Zucker shouts: *Please check my blood sugar, I could collapse into a coma at any time.* Rosa comes into the room, her face a shy question mark. Elisio thinks there's a mistake, he's confused, who's playing this joke on him, he makes a move to escape, he can't say anything, he just keeps staring at Rosa and he knows this is beyond all bounds of politeness. Franz, in order to break this strange silence and to answer Rosa's unasked question, says: *This gentleman has come here looking for a woman.* He indicates to Elisio to show her the photo, Rosa takes it and looks at it. Rosa: *But that's me!* Elisio's mouth makes a strange sound a *tss* or *kchch*, while his shoulders jump up and his head is about to nod. But Franz remains calm: N*o, she killed herself, she was lying in the refrigeration room on my first day at Berger's, you can't have known her.* And yet Rosa looks like a dead woman and a dead woman can look like Rosa; Rosa feels her throat, Rosa's trying to see if she can still speak, Rosa can speak, she says: *Killed.* She says it as if it's something someone still has to prove, as if it's not at all certain, but Franz knows for sure: *Yes, she drowned, at the docks.* Franz doesn't like talking about these things at home, he wants the dead to belong to him and Elisio says nothing any more. Elisio is simply a heartbeat. And Rosa has to make sure again: *But she looks like me!* She looks from Franz, who does not return her gaze, to Elisio, whom she doesn't know and has never seen before and she doesn't know how he came to have her photo: *But that's me!* She holds the photo out to him, a question, a criticism, an accusation, a verdict of guilt, a judgement; a judgement that Elisio has been waiting for the whole time, maybe even hoping for and Elisio takes the photo and says: *Yes, it's you.*

17. ELLA III

Helmut, ELLA's husband, has a goldsmith's magnifier in his eye and is busy making something very small with his hands. The television shows a speech by the President. ELLA watches with the sound off.

ELLA   He makes jewellery,

day after day, pound after pound.

Rings.

For years he's only made

rings.

Who wants all these rings,

hopeless circles without a beginning or end

and above all no way out.

I don't know.

Nothing else any more.

Rings.

From cheap nickel, from brass copper plastic platinum

silver gold, with and without stones, engraved round the edge

twisted around themselves several times or

plain metal bands without decoration,

and so on,

sometimes he puts one through another

like links in a chain,

as if he's hoping

for a magic trick one day

that one day both these prisoners

will one day be released from each other

but one day, darling,

we're going to have to do that ourselves,

because, being non-believers, there's no

words of redemption going to help us.

She is about to clip him on the back of the head, but pauses and instead makes a gesture of tenderness.

You don't want to hurt me

but you do.

The mere fact

that you exist,

 you jewel,

practically kills me.

Silence.

My book about

The Unreliable World, I quote:

'We attempt to find an explanation for events
around us, for our lives, for the happenings of the
world ex post facto, in the hope that if we can apply
these universal rules, we might influence the future.
But these causal links are only ever apparent in
retrospect and no one, neither us, nor God, nor
even nature itself possesses any knowledge about
how we will develop together. We might as well
throw dice.'

Pause.

He doesn't understand,

the President.

There is no fate

other than what we ourselves decide.

But as we cannot know

in what direction our decisions lead

we are blind

regarding ourselves,

aren't we, Helmut.

Tender gesture.

Retrospectively of course

we like to explain everything

by our own free will

so that we don't feel like animals,

don't we, Helmut.

Gives him a clip on the back of the head.

The small steps and the big ones.
You, the manual worker,
seeing cause and effect
in practice every day.
If the metal's too hot
it runs away from you.
Have I said today
how much I hate you.

Is about to give him a clip on the back of the head, but stops and instead makes a tender gesture.

Satisfied.
I'm never satisfied.
It would contradict my work ethic.
Satisfaction would even destroy my existence,
or at least deprive it of any basis,
and as I cannot progress further than my work progresses –
what am I saying what am I saying
what am I thinking,
I work therefore I am me.

Silence.

I'm not giving in.
I'm going to start again from the beginning,
one more time,
go back to the beginning
to
A.
move my arse one last time
as sexily as possible,
of course.
A

For
A
for
appropriate

Silence.

appropriate
I don't know
I can't imagine anything
appropriate any more
at my age being
appropriate is more appropriate

Pause.

poverty
oh Helmut
oh dear
all my courage is gone
all my anger even
all my fire

Silence.

no consolation
any of it

Silence.

Hits HELMUT on the back of the head until he falls across the table, bloody and dead.

18. THE UNRELIABLE WORLD

ABSOLUTE, FADOUL, ELISIO, FRAU HABERSATT and FRAU ZUCKER. Some time after ABSOLUTE's operation. In the centre, money.

FADOUL	So.
FRAU HABERSATT	So.
ELISIO	So.
FRAU ZUCKER	Leave her alone.
ABSOLUTE	Nothing. Absolutely nothing. Ha Ha.
FRAU ZUCKER	Now you leave her alone.
ABSOLUTE	I can see –
FADOUL	Yes –
FRAU HABERSATT	Yes –
ELISIO	Yes –
ABSOLUTE	I can see sounds. I can hear what I'm supposed to see. It hurts so much.
FADOUL	It takes time. It might last a while. You need to do your exercises.

Silence.

FADOUL	There's even some left over.
ELISIO	God's money.
FRAU ZUCKER	Anyone else want an operation.
FADOUL	Anyone else with an unfulfilled desire.
ELISIO	Yes, how can we become legal. How do the dead come to life.
FADOUL	Now stop that. Just stop it. Go home.
ELISIO	Home where. The tower. And then. Jump off the roof?
FRAU HABERSATT	A giant cockroach is sitting on his liver crying over the world.
ELISIO	Why am I bitter. Why. *(Waves around in front of ABSOLUTE's face, who notices nothing.)* So.
FADOUL	So.

FRAU HABERSATT	So.
ABSOLUTE	What is it.
FRAU ZUCKER	Still nothing.
ELISIO	Now you know. Senseless torture. A hope which turned out to be in vain.
FADOUL	It can take a while. Her eyes have got to get used to things.
FRAU HABERSATT	Her brain has to get used to things.
FRAU ZUCKER	The whole person has to get used to things. I stand up sometimes on both legs and then suddenly I fall over and only then do I remember –
ABSOLUTE	*(To FADOUL.)* I feel sick. I feel dizzy. There's an anthill growing in my head. I'm walking around as if I'm on a ship, I can see vague circles and light patches and sometimes something that could be a colour but it has no silhouette. And I can't recognize either you or Elisio.
FADOUL	I can tell you why. I can tell you exactly why.
FRAU ZUCKER	I used to be blessed with the eyes of a hawk, sharp as a blade, clear as a mountain stream and shining like crystal in the sunlight. But the sight of those eyes of mine dissolved like a sugar lump in tea. Yes, sugar. *Pause.* If I was an eagle –
ABSOLUTE	My brain can't get used to it.
ELISIO	Give it time.
FRAU HABERSATT	Patience and practice. You have to do your exercises. Fadoul is right about that.

Pause.

FADOUL	What are we going to do with the money.

Silence.

ELISIO	It's your money, Fadoul. None of us wants it.
FRAU HABERSATT	If I was you, I'd save it.
FADOUL	For whom. For when.

FRAU ZUCKER	What do you mean save it, spend it, as long as you've got two legs and have no worries.
Silence.	
FADOUL	*(To ABSOLUTE.)* It's not progressing because you have no belief. You're a non-believer and treat God like dirt. You believe in doctors and science but not in the power of God and that's why he can do nothing for you and it's all your fault.
ELISIO	What do you expect, a miracle.
FADOUL	No not a miracle, not a fucking miracle, though God could create that too, because he can do everything, but you treat him with contempt, that's why he sends you no happiness; why did he send me the bag, why me? Out of all the worthless illegals and outsiders and homeless, why me, did you ever think about that?
ELISIO	Maybe because you're a saint, Fadoul? Maybe because you've never done anything unjust? Maybe because it was a useful act to watch a woman drown without lifting your divine fingers? Maybe that fucking bag is your fucking reward?
FADOUL	*(Demonstrates that he is able to control himself.)* What I expect is that she will pray and work with us, not a miracle, not a miracle, I'm only expecting her to pray a little bit and co-operate –
FRAU ZUCKER	Dear Herr Fadoul, that's exactly what I keep saying to my phantom pains: please, phantom pains, co-operate with the rest of my body and go away.
FADOUL	I understand, I understand. *(Packs the money into the bag.)* What more do you want me to do for you. I give you presents, I give you money, I open the world for you. I bring light. All you need to do is tell me what you want, believe in me and be patient, – *(Pause.)* Absolute, make an effort, make a bit of an effort, for my sake – please.

ABSOLUTE	Noises, Fadoul. Bright, colourful circles. And that's all.
FADOUL	Can't you or don't you want to! See! See!
ABSOLUTE	Don't, Fadoul, let go – I can't see you, I can't see you.
FADOUL	Nice party here. You're traitors, you're cowards, let you lose all hope for ever – But me, I'm cheerful. I am so cheerful. It's the money makes me so cheerful. The money even makes me happy. Even without you. *(Takes the money and leaves.)*

Silence.

ABSOLUTE	If each of you had another wish, here, now, what would you ask for?
FRAU ZUCKER	If I worked at a petrol station –
FRAU HABERSATT	I'd like – . I'd like – .

Silence.

FRAU HABERSATT	I'd like to run a mobile library. I would only have freshly printed books with new pages which I could inhale while sleeping. I would give lifts to every hitchhiker I liked. They would have to read to me and when I got tired of their voice I would drop them at the edge of the road. I wouldn't be clingy any more, never again. I would think about myself, I would forget about young people. I would be a – bird migrating.
FRAU ZUCKER	If I worked in a petrol station – don't laugh at me. I like the smell of petrol. I would sit somewhere way out in the country next to my lone pump dreaming of the cars as they drove past. – Sometimes I'd stick rude leaflets under their windscreen wipers. I would deliver fuel and the danger of fire. – And from time to time I would go a hundred metres down the street or into the next field or on top of a hill, far enough anyway, to smoke a cigarette. In perfect peace.

Silence.

But sometime, when my time was come, I would push my bed next to the pump, in a great puddle of petrol; I would smoke a cigarette and fall into a coma and then there would be an immense explosion of sugar –

Silence.

ELISIO   Absolute?

ABSOLUTE   Me – I would go back to the Blue Planet. To its complete world, its golden red light and the haze of the men who've come from work and quickly combed through their hair and washed under their armpits with rosemary soap. I'd dance again. What else am I supposed to do.

Silence.

ELISIO   Me –
        I'd like to be a lifeguard.

19. IN FRONT OF THE SEA THAT FILLS THE HORIZON II

ROSA goes for a walk in front of the sea that fills the horizon. She is carrying an umbrella. She walks up and down by the water's edge, just once. She puts down the umbrella, without folding it up, the wind blows it into the water, the waves carry it away. She undresses slowly, places her clothes carefully together one after another in a neat pile, as if she is putting them in a cupboard. Her movements are fluid and concentrated. She leaves the pile behind her. She goes into the future.

LAND WITHOUT WORDS

This translation of *Land Without Words* was commissioned by the Royal Court Theatre and first produced by suite42 at The Caves/Just The Tonic as part of the Edinburgh Festival Fringe on 3rd August 2009 with the following team:

Performance   Lucy Ellinson

Direction   Lydia Ziemke
Design   Claire Schirck
Original Sound   Owen Lasch
Light Design   Victor Egea

I

and when people ask me
what was it like

well
well
well
what was it like

then I say
nothing
and if they're pushy
go on
then I think
what do I think about

if I was a painter
just supposing
it would be easier
question

could I say

in the past
for far too long
bodies were important
for a while they were fitting
then replaceable
ultimately insignificant
bodies sometimes naked sometimes not
in manically magnified detail
with all their wounds scars stitches reddened orifices
bodies the shade of rotten salmon
but the texture more like pork hide fat gristle
every sinew clearly visible
this emphasis on inevitable decay
was fashionable for a long time still gets used now

the human body made monstrous to reveal its poverty
so it can be comforted

that was a phase of mine
then I thought
when every doctor is superior to a painter
in the precision of their case histories or their anatomy
at least I can paint broken ragged amputated
that's what I did next it's a long time ago
move on quickly keep moving on the mistakes have
already been paid for the wound the
shame in my heart mall round visible forever like the
cigarette someone
once put out on your skin
that's enough memories
(breaks off)

and to a new
creating a role instead of talking about yourself

basically a declaration of bankruptcy
doubled
hiding in words
behind colours
as if that was easier
if I was a painter

question
and to a new don't
give up
and to a new don't
question yourself
don't let yourself
be questioned
(laughs)
keep on painting
(breaks off)

or this craving for beauty
that no one'll admit
what's really beautiful
the smell of a friend for example
with their own very distinct armpit sweat
and immediately the question arises again
how do you paint that
or a square yard of pavement
peach stone half a shoeprint
splash of paint broken glass
petrol stain twig with three leaves
and now
no frame just hang it on the wall
bang it's art
more than that
that is beauty
just need to change the angle of perception a bit

that's what I was thinking
before I came to k.
and I'd tried out a couple of things
without really getting anywhere

all I could do were surfaces
a lot of pretty surfaces

what was underneath
I couldn't get what was underneath
I thought I would know what it was
but I didn't

but I was determined
to keep on

and then afterwards
(breaks off)

you know this painter
R. the one I'm most in awe of

someone once said about him
he was making an environment
where your whole spirit becomes isolated
that's it
and then
you just have to deal with it
he helped you deal with yourself*

I'm not interested in provocation
but where's the pain

...

and the joy
(breaks off)

you know this painter
R. the one I'm most in awe of
someone once said about him
he was making an environment
where your whole spirit becomes isolated
but that's not it at all
as an objective that's totally wrong
the opposite is correct what's got to be attempted is
where your whole spirit connects to everything
if it didn't sound so pseudo-populist
and how
do you ever
ok then
resignation

...

question

and the joy

---

*   *cf. Brice Marden, Interview by Mark Rosenthal, 19. September 1997, in: Jeffrey Weiss (ed.): Mark Rothko, Yale University Press, New Haven and London 1998*

all objects everything suggestive of meaning must
be abandoned all forms must be abandoned I
was convinced of that because every single thing
immediately gets loaded with so much meaning if so a
while all you paint are hazelnut branches then it means
aha back to nature like the object is really important
and it is of course but not per se cézanne needed his
apples and pears not because he was a fruit painter
but because he was using paint to investigate the
spatial properties of a table with stuff on top of it and
then outdoors it was about light, how it changes the
surroundings, whole decades the same mountain and of
course it is the same but it's not identical haha
now for what's pleasing but first a digression a question
I hate why are there so few really good female painters
I can't explain to be honest I've never really been
interested in any event there seem to be so few really
good female painters that people have had to make
special catalogues about them called women in art and
they get their own exhibition where there's always
at least one georgia o'keeffe which is bound to be a
petunia and not the bleached animal skull in the desert
why
it's about a feeling of well-being
petunia on this side skull with horns on that side
what do people feel when they look at the petunia that's
more pleasing than how they react to seeing the skull
it baffles me
as far as I'm concerned the petunia's a thousand times
less pleasing than the animal skull why the petunia's
too beautiful too perfect and that means the whole
picture is lying to you it's lying to you so much I could
run away screaming the whole picture's smiling so
falsely right in your face look how soft and easy life is
the petunia's like a supermodel image of life and it's got
this erotic charge to it it makes me want to throw up
but people like it
counter suggestion

the principle's like this you put an animal carcass in a
glass case with ants for example
you make sure there's sufficient oxygen supply and
watch the ants go about their work
ok it's been done brackets damien hirst
what I'm interested in
is making a colour picture of that
surface surface surface nothing concrete
anything recognizable disappears
deer carcass red ants yellow the bones grey
then I call the whole thing no.19 and the gallery can
add on red yellow grey
afterwards nobody's ever going to hit on
the fact that it's a hundred thousand ants devouring a
dead deer
but anyone standing in front of it is going to feel the
same feeling looking at this
picture that they would watching the real event
that's what matters
being able to paint like that
that's what I want to achieve
that's the goal
the disturbance the thrill the waves of stings and bites
the acid the flesh with holes emerging in it bilious
stinking numbing skin turf little eggs
finally clean bones
a living burial observed life cycle
at some point grass springs up in one corner
relief purity resurrection redemption
and all that in one big picture
red yellow grey
that is art

how overbearing that was
or just unreachable

and the pain
and if it was the last picture

I painted
and if it was the last thing
I had to say

I'm not interested in provocation
the pain
the pain's got to be there
always present
and the joy

III

yeah well that was all before I got to k.
I mean I was prepared for it
but then again not
and after that
then
well then I didn't know any more
I didn't know what
the point of it was any more
painting
(breaks off)

what can you paint
what can't you
everything's possible again
everything's impossible again

I can't forget the pictures
pictures you understand
not colours not surfaces nothing abstract
concrete
scenes
real scenes

and then
you are stuck

this incredible lead weight of exhaustion crushing your
body from the moment it sits up in bed in the morning

you are stuck
once you've been there

and people ask you
when are you getting out
not
when are you going back
to the place

you came from no
when are you getting out

I don't know if I'll ever be able to get out

one night in k. I dreamt I'd chopped off my right
thumb, index and middle fingers, one after another
with a little sharp axe it just happened the fingers were
sewn up cleanly a flap of skin like a cap placed over the
stumps it didn't hurt but it was a very strange feeling
only having two fingers left or not having three the
three most important the three grip fingers any more
it's almost as if your whole hand is missing
does that mean I can't paint any more does that mean I
can't paint any more
(breaks off)

wake up wake up
wake up

the world goes round so fast or rather the earth goes
round so fast and the world goes round with it
said the man who came back from the war and now sits
in a wheelchair

when people ask me
if I want to change anything
(breaks off)

before
when people used to ask me
if I wanted to change anything
by painting
I said yes
I think so
even if it's just one person
one single viewer at whatever moment

for example
I said

for the picture
it's simply about
being there
being there independently
not questioning anything
allowing everything validity or everything you are
it doesn't question you when you look at it
it leaves you a way in it gives you room

war doesn't happen in a picture
what you experience
that's what counts
there's nothing else to understand

you've got to dare to do things
sometimes you're going to make a fool of yourself
doing them
but there again
you only ever dare do something
if you're daring to make a fool of yourself

you've seen the surface
pretty much the surface
but you feel what's beneath
you know it
don't you

and even saying that is making a fool of yourself
and there's no way out of this trap
there's only

and to a new

the club owner says to me so you've come to k. to
paint something about the city have you any idea yet
what that might be I could hang one in my club I hold
my breath for a moment and tell him well I think I'll
probably paint the rabbits that hop through the grass
in this chic ghostly oasis of yours or your gorgeous
swimming pool in the afternoon with the boys in front
of it sipping their gin and tonics and let it look like
a fucking hockney only the boys are missing an arm
or a leg or a head because they trod on some fucking
mine before they could learn how to swim is that what
you've got in mind

he considered briefly and then actually said but there
are no land mine victims in our club and I laugh not
very loud

if I could paint the mountains maybe the massive
mountain ranges we fly over for hours driving through
them for hours on end blowing up mines I couldn't
begin to imagine now I can hear it right up close mined
areas left and right of the road stones that are red stones
that are white mined areas cleared areas clay buildings
with white signs chopped off the shepherds drive their
animals in in and away when the sun comes up the
men shape their hands into shallow bowls, pour out
light with them and wash their faces two or three times
they let the water run over their faces holy light the
men carry weapons

another night in k. I dreamt about a man blond short
curly hair bare chest who lives with a tiger in a large
empty open space a concrete arena like the airport in
k. in the far distance there's a fence running round the
grounds (the man doesn't look like a fighter not like a
soldier and the tiger is a tiger) it's hot there are clouds
hanging in the sky and shadows fall onto the concrete
will he tame him will he tame him I watch them both
but have no feelings either way

the soldiers the patrols the dust the fat-tailed sheep and
day and night the stink of shit everywhere you go it
never leaves you you feel dirty the whole time like you
can't get enough air to begin with I'd wake up in the
night with my t-shirt ripped open afraid of suffocating
the dryness you dry up slowly from the inside

four children sit on the steeply sloping street their
father's next to them all on their haunches trying with
their bare hands to catch what little water there is
running downhill as if they were on a mountain stream
further up there's a goat urinating in the gutter in the
bazaar two women are arguing over a carpet synthetic
with an embossed pattern a boy offers almond sweets
on a tray piled up into a pyramid a knife blade the
sound of a melon exploding makes everyone turn
round

wake up wake up
wake up

it smells of disinfectant of sunburn of blood of diesel a
swarm of electric generators the buzz of metal hornets
behind sandbag barricades the ventilator whisks up
the heat boots kicking the barrack door shut every few
minutes and the doctor in her uniform bends over me
so you have come to k. to do some paintings don't
breathe now the infusion drips slowly into my arm
don't breathe
days go by like this weeks months
without breathing
the heat seeps into our bodies
the earth the air the water the smell the language
you get sick from breathing this air
so that was it
that wasn't even the start

you've seen the surface
pretty much the surface
but you feel what's beneath
you know it
don't you

creating a white
that reflects your own fear
a white with no way out
bright blinding intolerable like vertical sunlight at
midday
a white that makes you close your eyes when you look
at it
and when you've closed them the
light keeps working
under your eyelids and gives
you a headache and you think you can
smell the heat the heat before it
it singes your lips your flesh before
it scorches your skin
the light just before it
explodes

she turns up one afternoon first a few steps behind me
then slowly overtaking I can see her out of the corner
of my eye she can only be eight judging by her height
a man's walking next to her the man sticks his hand
out points to her he talks at me quietly stubbornly I
look at him the girl should keep walking shocked I try
not to let my shock show the two of them circle round
me surround me one on the right one on the left then
both on the same side again sometimes they hang back
a little and every time I think they've gone the man's
insistent speech is in my ear his hand open in front of
me I could stand still we could communicate with each
other in sign language eyes hands but shame drives
me on the girl is now running constantly by my side
she won't give up she's never going to let go of me
she's going to accompany me anywhere I try to escape
and when do you get out never never never again she
tugs at my sleeve at my elbow a tiny unyielding bird
persecuting me and brings her hand up to her face
to her mouth so that without wanting to I look at her

every time the man has knocked her headscarf off her
arms are bare her skull is bald the skin on her head
on both arms is burnt her face is burnt her skin is dark
red almost brown without a wisp of hair and full of
tiny creases as if she'd been wrapped in the skin of a
baby elephant her eyelashes singed off and not a single
tooth in her open mouth she looks like an old woman
she doesn't speak she looks at me blankly she has light
brown eyes and with one finger she points again and
again and again into her wrenched open toothless
mouth out of which she sticks a swollen tongue towards
me

where your whole spirit becomes isolated

black and brown
when the lack of courage comes back when
fear catches up with me
the wish to be invisible
to get lost
in what I do

to say nothing
(breaks off)

another day
twenty men and one woman
at the end all the men have gone
and I'm alone with her
during the war she was in exile
she's written 17 novels and
1 autobiography
none of it was published
she hid the manuscripts
she's 63 years old
and only speaks when she's told to

no one wants a life like that
no one wants to identify with someone like that

a life like that nobody
wants you don't want to identify yourself with someone
like that no one's willing to do that and I'm not either
I've got nothing at all in common
with her
mute
I'm not like that
question
question
question
hacked down into silence
that's not what I want to be
in any other life

in a
land without words
(breaks off)

creating a white
square even surface
that runs out of focus at the edges
doesn't want to divide itself clearly
to end abruptly
a white
stopped along its lowest edge by
a thin yellow line
and on its top edge by a rather wider red one
and both lines would not be at all straight
but would run out a little shakily
inserted freehand into the run off of white paint
horizontally through the middle a black line
that casts a grey shadow above and below

I'd call it
girl with tongue and skin and fire
WITHOUT WORDS

you've seen the surface

pretty much the surface
but you feel what's beneath
you know it
don't you
and listen to them the giggling chatting breathing loud
the painted hands ornaments in red on the inner
surfaces
the top sides of the fingers
eyes edged in black
before we land in paris they go to the toilet
they take off everything their veils and shawls they
change all their clothes
they put on high heels and earrings lipstick and do their
nails
my neighbour whispers and strokes my arm
which is now bare
and when they come out
they are very very sexy
very very sexy
he says nothing
and now
you are stuck
once you've been there
you will always want to get back
and stay
you stay

the painter I'm most in awe of
of course it keeps changing
but the painter I'm most in awe of
now and always
he
(breaks off)

in the end he had very bad depression and
he had treatment but
I don't think that was the reason

his pictures got darker they say
I don't agree about that
he used darker colours
brown on brown
black on brown
all of it hung in the most confined space
with practically no daylight
and still
the pictures glow
the colours glow
they shine from within
a black that shines from within
you've got to imagine that
as if a light had suddenly appeared in the darkest forest
(long silence)

yeahitskitschyiknow

he
one night he
cut open his veins
and bled to death

I think

I think he had

he had no more pictures
you understand

once you've been there
you are stuck
and you'll always want to get back

and the pain
and the joy

now I'm out and
sit in front of my walls
stand up and turn the music off so
there's peace at last and I
can hear the silence
the wind in the desert
the dogs howling at night in the streets
now I'm back and
look at the window frame for hours at a time
don't put the light on and
when it gets dark
I go to bed some time
with my eyes open
and wait for the heat to press down on me
(Breaks off)

and when people ask me how it was

...

well well well well
you're stuck
and you'll always want to get back

I can't find the white
all I can find is
dark red brown black
brownbrownblackred
wood fire ashes
desert footsteps explosion
sky lightning hell

I wanted to paint the light

clay houses slipping down the cliff streets closed army
charred ruins goats looking for food among the rubbish
and faeces on dried up river beds a shrouded beggar

woman is given a banknote a boy pulls her veil he
claws at her hand he wants to take her money away
she screams he hits her she falls kicks out at him the
banknote rips in two the boy runs away with one half
she huddles on the ground under the sky blue pleated
folds of her veil that form a fan around her a fanned
dome a human being under a cloth a cover or maybe
it's a cat someone's already tricked into a bag she can
sense it all and keeps stock still one more breath before
they tie up the bag and throw her into the river to
drown

I admire
what he painted
how he managed to free himself
from everything
images scenes
ballast
someone said about him
he was making an environment
where your whole spirit becomes isolated
that's it
and then
you just have to deal with it

you have to deal with yourself

I'm not interested in provocation
but where's the pain

...

and the joy